Uncomplicating Your Life

Simple Truths That Can Change Everything

Anthony Fernando

Kings Park, Winnipeg

Copyright © 2015 by Anthony Fernando ~ Your Best Shot

All rights reserved. No part of this book may be reproduced in any form or by any electronic or mechanical means, including information storage and retrieval systems, without permission in writing from the author, except by a reviewer who may quote brief passages in a review.

Web site www.uncomplicatingyourlife.com
        www.AnthonyJFernando.com

Fernando, Anthony
Uncomplicating Your Life
.
ISBN 978-0-9919458-0-1

Publisher: Anthony J. Fernando Your Best Shot
Book design concept and layout: Segun Olude
Editor: Anna Olsen
Cover design by Anthony Fernando
Photos and text: Anthony Fernando

What is the measure of a Life?

To me the love and intent with which you live your life is the most important legacy you can enrich this earth with. My mom thought that she did not accomplish a lot in her life and I took it as a challenge to show her how many lives she's enriched.

Words can only attempt to explain what and who a person is. But we are so much more, and while we do not always use all of our abilities, how we are with others defines our life. She was loving to everyone she met. Her kindness reached beyond her material possessions, she gave of herself.

I will miss hearing her voice and being in her company, but I know that who she is, was not the body she inherited, but the spirit that lived with that body.

I know I only have to think about her and she is with me. I know that love doesn't end with death but carries on forever. I know that as much as she has been a peaceful person, she is now so much more at peace.

The beauty of her spirit continues to live on in all the lives she touched. Her ability to affect others in her own quiet and caring manner changed the lives of others. I know it changed mine, and I'm glad I had the opportunity to let her know that, and feel blessed to have been a part of her life.

To my MOM I love you always.

Dedicated to the memory of **Sybil D. Fernando**
January 19th. 1931 - November 20th, 2005

Contents

On a Spiritual Path ... Living the Light Within

Introduction	3
Healing In Difficult Times	11
A Smile	15
I Asked ... And God Responded	17
Appreciation	23
My Vision for Myself	27
Remembering our True Selves	31
Feelings: The Voice of our Spirit	33
The Illusion of Fear	35
Trust	39
We Are God's In formation	45

Inner Peace ... Living in your Light

Accepting Change	51
Accepting Truth	53
Awareness	57
Believing in Myself	61
Self Confidence	67
Imagine Life into Being	71
The Power of Fear	73
How Judgment Creates Conflict	77
Free Will	81
My Gift	83
What is Reality?	85
The Dis-ease of Being Right	87
The Truth can Set us Free	91
We are All Magnificent	95
Why am I Hurting?	97
Who am I ?	99
We Must Heal How we Feel	103
This Insignificant Voice	105

Life ... Experiencing the Divine in All

Allowing	109
Boundaries	113
Expectations	117
Being	121
What do I feel I am Missing?	123
Life	127
Re-mind Yourself	129
An Honourable Life	133

Creating with Love ... A Path to the Divine Within

Creating A Life Of Love	137
To my Cherished One with Love	139
The Gift of Love	141
What does it mean to Love Unconditionally?	147
Communicating with Love	150

Prayers ... Communicating with Love

What is Prayer?	**151**
Prayer for Divine Love	153
Prayer for Self Acceptance	153
Prayer to know the God Within	153
Prayer for Living Spiritually	155
Prayer for Accepting Change	155

Acknowledgements

Neale Donald Walsh & Anthony Fernando

To my mom (Millicent), for her guidance and her unwavering love. Also for teaching me to cook, sew and iron. She said it was important to learn these things so I didn't have to rely on a woman to take care of me.

To my mom (Sybil), for the grace and love with which she lived her life. I thank her for standing up and defending me even when she knew it was dangerous to do so. Although she is no longer of this earth, her caring and love live on.

To my son Spencer, who has grown up to be a man I can look up to, thanks for your support and love.

To my editor Anna Olson, for challenging me on my ideas and concepts. This has helped me learn, understand and grow.

To Nathalie Kleinschmit, thanks for your encouragement, expertise, and a great biography. You've helped me see myself in a new light.

To the women in my life who have each taught me something new about myself, especially the shadow areas of my personality that I was blind to.

To my friends. Although my family is small and fragmented, you have embodied the idea that 'Friends are the family we choose" – Dr. Wayne Dyer.

To Neale Donald Walsh whose books came into my life at a time I needed to hear their messages the most, and for giving me the title to this book.

To the men in our healing group. Each week your courage shows through and I am blessed to be part of your growth. Thank you for being such a strong catalyst in my own.

With Blessings.

Introduction

We all have gifts and talents that are meant to be used to make a meaningful contribution to our co-creation of life with our fellow beings. When we feel fear, we create experiences that do not measure up to our inner knowing of how enriching life can be. Our contributions are minimized because we doubt ourselves.

I believe all our fears are given birth through doubt. When we doubt ourselves we create experiences using a small portion of our energy. Our energy is infinite but if we fear that our goal is not possible, then we dissipate a lot of that energy.

We create our experiences with thoughts based on either love or fear. *It is much easier to create with love, except when we've become so accustomed to the look of fear its face is familiar to us.* Most of our experiences are created out of habit. With each encounter, we search our minds for similar experiences from our past, and using this as a basis, we re-create similar experiences. Creating based on past influences robs us of our personal power, which can only be applied in the present.

Our personal power is infinite.

The most challenging periods in life usually offer the most growth, and these experiences can help us remember the essence of who we are. We are creative beings weaving the tapestry of our lives with each choice we make. Our quality of life is shaped by our belief in our power to create.

The power within can only be diminished by our belief in our ability to use that power. If we believe our power is limited then we only use the amount we believe we have. Likewise, when we believe we have lots of personal power, we exude that belief in the way we speak, the way we move and the way we feel.

Choices create reality.

External influences can direct our choices when we resist the guidance from the intuitive part of our being. Our intuition or gut feelings can guide us to create experiences that reflect the most positive longings of our soul. While we may not know the outcome of our choices, our ability to be open to the change it brings will guide us effortlessly in living the life we desire. We experience the pain of our choices when we resist the result of those choices. We experience suffering when we continue to make the same choices we have in the past yet still resist the reality we create from those choices. Every choice we've made has contributed to the reality we experience in the present. With hindsight, we can see the patterns that make up who we are today.

As a teenager I began reading self-help books, and one of the first I can remember was Psycho-Cybernetics by Dr. Maxwell Maltz. He explained the workings of our mind, and how we perceive our reality based on what we believe. Our reality IS our perception of the world coloured by how we feel. We each use a different brush and different colours. So while the underlying foundation (life) is the same, we each paint it differently.

As an adult I discovered The Four Agreements by don Miguel Ruiz. It is a simple four-step guide to a living a life of peace, a copy of which I keep on my desk.

1. Be impeccable with your word.
2. Don't take anything personally.
3. Don't make assumptions.
4. Always do your best.

Another of his books "Mastery of Love" helped remind me of the importance of loving unconditionally. We've been taught that love comes with a price. Thus our experience of love is usually based on the actions of others, distorted by their personal beliefs and not our own inner guidance.

When I was 44 years old I experienced the most difficult period in my life. My wife and I separated and what caused the most difficulty was realizing that the image I had in my mind about our relationship was much different than hers. I felt adrift, without direction, in a way I can best describe as being in an ocean of despair.

It was then I was determined to start looking for answers, and to truly understand the purpose of my existence. I would drop off my son at school and find sanctuary in our local conservatory, a place in nature that gave me a moment of peace I couldn't find at home. As difficult as life was at the time, I realized sometimes change is forced upon us so we can recognize that we are more than we are allowing ourselves to be. For that reason, I've been thankful for the experience, and learned to receive it as an opportunity to allow my spirit more expression in my life.

Each relationship since then has helped me recognize something else about myself. For example:

- It isn't fair to have expectations of others based on my personal needs.
- To truly live, I must allow the people in my life to choose their own destiny and not take their comments and actions personally.
- I must allow others the freedom to fully express themselves at all times, even if that includes me not being a part of their lives.

- It's easy to be centered and have inner peace when alone but the challenge is doing so within a relationship.
- I learned that as much as we would like it to be otherwise, it's the difficulties we face that makes life worth living. It's like music; without silence between the notes, music loses its beauty and becomes noise. So it is with life, our challenges help us experience life more fully than when everything seems to be operating smoothly.
- I've also realized we must learn to embrace our difficulties because they help remind us of our creative abilities, and gives us the opportunity to re-create our life experiences.
- Because a relationship doesn't last doesn't mean it didn't work.

It was at this time I discovered the Conversations with God books by Neale Donald Walsch. I had found a "truth" that mirrored how I felt inside. I consider these some of the most profound set of books I've ever read on spirituality and God, and in some ways this was what my bible could be. Yet, even though I'd read the bible many times, I've been careful not to make it or any particular book the only truth. The true ability of profound works is to ignite the spark within that guides us to finding the divine within ourselves, and more importantly, experiencing God in each experience.

One night after a particularly difficult day with my ex-wife, I decided I would have my own "Conversation with God." I asked, "Why isn't my life working? Why is life so difficult? Why do I allow the words of others to influence how I feel about myself?" I needed answers and was prepared to sit for as long as it took. Almost immediately, the words expressed in "I asked...and God responded," came to me.

Here is a sample: "The answers are within dear one. They always are. The moment you ask the question the answer already exists. In whatever you do, whatever you feel there it is. You do not have to wait for me, you decide; That is how God experiences a human existence - through you. The reason you feel the way you do is because you do not trust yourself. That is your downfall, feeling you have to wait for my guidance. It is not my guidance you seek but your own. Look inside yourself."

I believe there is an energy that exists in everything and everyone. This energy never dies, it never fades, it changes form. Our thoughts use this energy to create our experiences and possessions for the expression of our being. I believe we are each a part of this energy doing what energy does – create.

I also believe this energy is light. Quantum Physics explains it as extremely tiny strings of light that oscillates, vibrates, and changes form according to the observer.

If you believe the messages in the bible come from God consider what is written in John 12:36. Jesus states "While ye have light, believe in the light, that ye may be children of light." He considers himself as a light unto the world. "I am come a light into the world, that whosoever believeth on me should not abide in darkness." (John 12:45)

Jesus also says, "Verily, verily, I say unto you, he that believeth on me, the works that I do shall he do also; and greater works than these shall he do; because I go unto the Father." (John 14:12)

I interpret these messages to mean that we are capable of great things when we believe in and accept the light within us and our world. If we choose this belief, we then view everyone we meet and everything we experience as God expressing himself/herself/itself in a different form, and we will automatically treat ourselves and others with respect and love. We accept them without judgment in whatever way they present themselves, which they do with every action, every word, and every thought.

At times I've read what I've written and thought, Where did that come from? I realize at certain times in our lives, we open ourselves and allow the divine within us to more fully express its presence. We become more aware of a higher connection and utilize this to bring answers to the questions and challenges we face.

Although I use the word God, I realize the word God evokes strong emotions. It is my choice, however equally powerful are the words, UNIVERSAL ENERGY, DIVINE ENERGY, LOVE, LIGHT and LIFE. If you feel challenged using the word God, I ask that you substitute the above words or any other word you are more comfortable with as the word is not as important as the feeling of comfort we may have from experiencing God, Love, Energy, Light and Life in each moment.

In February 2007, I had lunch with Neale Donald Walsch (author of the Conversation with God books), and as our conversation progressed, he suggested I write a book. When I told him that I already had but it was not yet published he asked to read it. As he read it, he mentioned parts he thought was interesting in how the idea was presented. The working title at the time was Inspire Within, and when I said I was looking for a different title, he suggested using Uncomplicating Your Life: Simple Truths That Can Change Everything.

I offer the following with the hope that as you read this book you feel a connection to the divine spark within which I believe is a part of God that connects us to life and is always with us.

All the best, in Love and Light.

Las Cuevas Beach, Trinidad

On a Spiritual Path…
Living the Light Within

We are all on a spiritual path, some further along than others. There is no set route; we create our own with each choice we make.

Our choices are the left and right turns of our journey. This journey is not to a particular time or place, but a journey to fully recognizing the light within. It is in each one of us, and as we see it in ourselves we are then able to see it in others.

Our planet cannot exist without light. Life exists through the intricate combination of water, material and light. To appreciate the creativity of light in our lives we must also recognize and accept the absence of light, which we call darkness. Each exists within us for we are created in darkness and birthed in light.

We are "Beings of Light."

Assiniboine Park - Winnipeg, Canada

In each moment create how you choose to re-present yourself in the next moment by the choices you make in this one.

Healing In Difficult Times

The need to heal is based on an Illusion

Most of what we've been taught about life and the conclusions we've made are illusions. Our experiences have an impact on our lives based on the meaning we give them, yet the meaning we choose is usually formed from the opinions and beliefs of others.

We are all touched by the events we see unfolding worldwide and are affected in ways we may not fully understand. We see how quickly life can be lost and feel compelled to re-connect with what is truly important in life. The impact of local and worldwide events and times of difficulty may cause us to take time to reassess how we live and our purpose for living. In times of difficulty, families come together and are more likely to forgive each other for past transgressions. We realize that one of our most precious resources is love.

Although we seek healing when we experience discomfort in our bodies, this is only one form of healing. Lack of physical health is easier to recognize because we feel the dis-ease in our bodies. Likewise, emotional stress is easy to identify because we feel discomfort in how we relate to ourselves and others.

However, problems in our spiritual health are more subtle therefore more difficult to recognize.

So, how do we heal spiritually?

- *Forgive ourselves and others.* Try saying, "I accept responsibility for my life, releasing blame and judgment of others." In truth, no one causes us pain. There are only actions, and it's our perceptions and judgments that cause us pain, which can come from living through the expectations of others. This is one way we create suffering as part of our experience.

- *Find out what inspires us.* Inspiration awakens our strongest feelings, providing us with direction, purpose, and the energy to create. Creating is our gift, and our purpose in life.

Muriel Lake, Ontario

*When we live and act joyfully, our light becomes a beacon
for everyone we encounter.*

- *Go Within.* The inspiration to create comes from within. To feel inspired, we need to live "in-spirit." Living in-spirit means having faith in ourselves, and doing what brings us joy. When we live and act joyfully, our light becomes a beacon to everyone we encounter. Our joy can open a doorway which can shine light on a new path for others if they choose.

- *Use our free will.* We all have a magnificent tool called free will, which we use to create the life we desire. We create how we choose to re-present ourselves in the next moment by the choices we make in this one. Choose to create from a feeling of love and we will not have to feel badly for our choices. Choosing either consciously or unconsciously to create based on fear causes us to create outcomes that are not in alignment with our higher selves. If we do not like a choice we've made for any reason, we only have to cease making similar choices in the future. We do not need guilt, shame, envy or any other negative emotion to guide us. These types of emotions only makes us feel "bad" about ourselves, and limit the amount of energy we use to create.

- *Co-create with God.* We are co-creators of our lives with God, "The All That Is." If God is "All that is", are we not a part of all that which is God? We either live our lives as a part of God (love) or apart from God (fear). Our journey to healing our spirit, mind and body begins with remembering our true selves. (Substitute God with Higher Power, Universal Energy or whatever term aligns with your beliefs).

- *Re-member our true selves.* Member is defined as "a distinct part of a whole" or "one that belongs to a group or organization." Healing comes from re-membering, putting back together, rejoining the parts of ourselves that are not in harmony with nature and our divinity. We are all connected, we are all one; what we do for another, we do for ourselves.

- *Meditate, do yoga and exercise.* These are three ways that can help us reconnect to the loving energy available to us. Meditation gets us in touch with our spiritual essence, the part of us that is connected to Universal Energy. Yoga and similar exercises such as tai chi, qui gong etc., align our spiritual being with our physical self.

- *Give yourself permission to grow.* Love is the capacity to allow all other beings to grow into their fullest expression of self. We must give ourselves permission to do the same. This is where true love and healing begins.

This was written shortly after the World Trade Centre events on September 11th 2001 at the request of a magazine. I've included it because I believe the information is still relevant today. I consider it a tribute to a cousin that was working in one of the buildings at the time and was one of the over 3,000 people that lost their lives on that day.

We can brighten our world with just one smile.

A Smile

Deep inside I yearn for peace,
A little respite from my daily pressures,
The expectations of others.
I look into another's eyes
And see their pain, and in that moment forget my own.
But when I am alone and allow the busi-ness
Of the day to fall away, I feel
My insecurities, those moments of doubt.
I know I am more, beyond the mundane,
But yet it stays, this insecure feeling.
And then someone smiles and my day is brighter.
I know God has sent an angel, and if I listen
I hear the angelic voice,
If I look, I see the beauty,
If I smell, I smell the fragrance,
And if I open myself I feel the love.
In that one smile I am reminded that I am more,
More than I've allowed myself to be.
And even if I don't know,
Or don't remember God has,
For in each smile the face of God is shown to me,
An angel was sent just for me.
And I remember my love, my smile, my fragrance
Is also a light to another.
This is a truth, a light we can share with the world,
And we can brighten it with just one smile.

Manitoba Provincial Hwy. 330

In each moment share with the world the magnificence of who you are.

I Asked...
And God Responded

During an especially difficult time in my life, I felt I needed answers because my life wasn't working the way I would like. I remembered reading that God speaks to us but most of the time we do not listen. I decided I would ask God for answers and would listen as intently as possible. This is what came to mind.

The answers are within dear one. They always are. If you can ask the question the answer already exists. In whatever you do, whatever you feel, there it is, and you do not have to wait for me. You decide. That is how God experiences a human existence - through you. The reason you feel the way you do is because you do not trust yourself. That is your downfall, feeling you have to wait for my guidance. It is not only my guidance you should seek but your own.

Look inside yourself.

Then I said, "But I feel like I do ask and don't get answers."

Look all around you, determine what you wish to experience and live that. You sometimes hear my voice speaking through you, but because it seems so simple, so subtle, you wait for a loud voice. Listen to the voice within.

Stand up for yourself, declare to all the value of who you are, but most of all declare to yourself who you wish to be. But don't merely wish, you need to intend, and more importantly create. Create and re-create yourself in the highest and brightest image you can hold of who you are and what you can become. You are divine and holding yourself back and accepting any less is one of the biggest personal sins you can experience. Your life is given to you to create joy and love. Begin with self then all else is easy. It is then you realize that I do not direct your life but create for you the opportunity to create your own.

Manitoba Provincial Hwy. 330

Listen to the voice within

Therefore, don't wait for me, because the biggest joke is that I wait for you. I cannot help create with you that which you do not know. It is when you know what you desire that I bring to you the tools of the magician. With these tools you create life, not for others but for yourself.

So don't look to me for help until you decide what you want to create in your daily journey of life. Be aware and be determined, for out of these confidence is built, and with this confidence you marshal all the forces in the universe. These forces you call energy, and all energy combined forms me, and this is the energy you call God. And God wants what you want.

Little by little each day you take steps, small baby steps, but now it is time to make a quantum leap. Embrace yourself, love your self, and re-create yourself using your highest imagining possible. Intend the best and it will happen. To the extent you've developed your confidence, then it is to that level I can assist you. But make no mistake; I am not the creator of your experiences. You are; I am only the conduit. I created you with the power to create in your world based on the choices you make. In your daily life you create your experiences with the power you believe you have.

Let me explain: If you believe someone else has more power than you, you limit your own, and therefore will not utilize your incredible energy to live a life of your own choosing. You all want this yet few of you create it. Those who do you call special and gifted. But hear this, no one, no individual has more power than another. What needs to change in your vocabulary is your definition of power.

To God, power is the belief within each of you, of the amount of energy you have to create your own life experiences. No one is born with more or less than another. Your experiences are shaped by how much you believe you have, but that does not diminish the power itself.

It's like radio waves, all the signals and sounds are there, you need to be able to tune into the right frequency. You can tune in or tune out. That is your choice. However, the better choice for you is the one that brings you ultimately to joy and love.

Intend to create what you wish to experience and I guarantee you God will help. However, the road to your intention will not be the same one you've traveled thus far. You cannot travel the same road that got you here and have it take you someplace else.

Accept change.

Do not resist change, for if you intend something different, the familiar will not get you there. Holding on tightly (stubbornness) to a particular negative idea or belief shows up in your life as continually living the same negative experience (suffering). Resistance to change holds you back from the magic of daily living.

You are all part of nature and everything in nature changes. What is natural continually evolves. Decide to be from this moment on an evolving creator of life.

Be someone special to yourself and look to yourself always. No one else has the answers for you. That is your power, do not give it away, do not hoard it, use it. In each moment share with the world the magnificence of who you are. To create magic in your life, begin with the intention and a burning desire to know the creator within. This is the wellspring of magic and life. This is how you shape your experiences. Remember, no experience has any meaning except the meaning you give it.

No experience has any meaning except the meaning we give it.

Birds Hill Provincial Park, Manitoba

The energy that creates life is always available when we decide what we want to create.

Appreciation

The key to creating more positive life experiences.

God, if you were to speak to me of appreciation what would you say? How do I appreciate the parts of my life I feel are not working?

If you only expect to hear from me in certain ways you eliminate a lot of what I say in each moment. I speak to you always and in all ways. The problem is not do I communicate (for that is a better word), but are you open to recognizing how I communicate? When you say 'speak' you listen for a voice but we communicate in so many other ways.

Take for example your feelings. Your society places so little importance on feelings, entire generations grow up missing a very important part of themselves. Your feelings are your connection to the part of God that exists within you.

Let us look at love. You all have your own beliefs, thoughts, and ideas about love, but most of it is based on conditions. You question whether the love you seek is or will be in your life. Yet if you look around you there is an abundance of love but unless it is the way you want, you do not notice it.

To appreciate yourself and life, (one cannot exist without the other), accept without judgment all representations of love in your life. Know that as the creator of your world, love can always exist, and you will experience it to the level you feel yourself deserving of it. Change your perspective and you will change the way you experience life and love. Take time to notice that in each moment love exists.

Appreciate the love in your life using all of the marvelous gifts and talents you possess. Don't only look for love, but smell it, taste it, hear it and most of all feel it. Experience it with your entire being. Love even the so-called negative that happens in your life, for loving the negative is necessary before you can release it.

Make time for what you love. When you love, you are able to deal with difficulties which would normally defeat you. You do not have to look beyond your own experiences to know this. Your life is a testament to what you value and appreciate. Look around you beyond the material, and observe the people in your life. Some of you value material possessions more than people.

Whiteshell Provincial Park, Manitoba

Life is a testament to what we value and appreciate.

There is value in every experience, you only have to look beyond the experiences you consider negative to see there is beauty in all that occurs. Therefore give thanks for all your experiences, for it is all life.

With each experience decide whether to respond with love or fear. Your feelings represent the spirit within communicating with you. When you have a gut feeling your spirit is guiding you. Love can feel like an expansion of energy from within, while fear is restrictive and makes you feel like you have less energy to create a masterful life.

Life is energy. Love and fear are like two sides of the same coin. Both have the same creative energy directed in different ways. Look at what you fear and know they represent opportunities, unveiling the restrictions within to living and becoming the type of person you would like to be.

Love and fear are choices based on beliefs. Your beliefs form the foundation of your life experiences and are the starting point of your everyday creation.

You are always creating whether you believe you are or not. You are a magnificent creator, and a life filled with love lies beyond your fears.

Your fears are based on a prior judgment (yours or others) about an experience that is similar to what you now face. To create a new experience recreate yourself in this moment by changing your perspective about your prior experience. The energy that created the universe is available to you when you decide what you want to create.

Re-mind yourself that life is a process of creation and you have to decide what you wish to experience. For once you experience IT (whatever IT means to you) you'll recognize that the moment you know what you want, the universe aligns itself to help create it. However to change what has already been created, re-creation is necessary. In other words lighten up and create over, have a do-over but this time with love and joy as your guide.

Here is a method for getting more of what you desire. Write on a sheet of paper all you appreciate having in your life. List the people, places, activities and experiences that bring you joy. This builds a well-spring of positive energy which can then be the starting point of your next creation. When you make gratitude a regular part of your existence you cannot help but create more of what you consider good in your life. You will then realize that even in small amounts all you desire is already part of your life experience.

To be loving in each moment of now.

My Vision for Myself

A personal moment of reflection – reaching for a moment of peace during a difficult time in my life.

- I strive to be loving in each moment of now.

- I strive to appreciate all my experiences, those I judge as good and especially those I judge as bad. And, as I remember more of my personal power, I drop all judgment of myself and others experiencing life as it is presented.

- I will experience life as a series of choices I use to create my greatest vision of who I am.

- And who am I? I am a co-creator of my life with God.

- As I remember more of my power to create, my life changes.

- Negative experiences still happen, but my thoughts change, and I no longer judge anything or anyone. Therefore, I allow all life to be as it is, even as I allow myself to be. As I do this I create a life without needs or unreasonable expectations, allowing myself and others the divine right to be and to grow into our fullest expression of self.

- I hold love in my heart. And how do I do this? By loving myself. Through seeing the divine beauty in myself, I can then see it in others. This way I transform all my relationships, for all living beings are divine in their own right, no less or more than I.

Pisew Falls, Manitoba

Divinity cannot be controlled only experienced.

- I release control over my life by allowing myself to be. In each present moment, I allow myself to witness the perfection of all my life experiences.

- I release all pre-conceived notions of how my life should be, for I limit the magic in my life through trying to control the experiences I am a part of. Divinity cannot be controlled, only experienced.

- I listen to my heart, for only in listening to my heart can I achieve my highest accomplishments.

- I am held in the loving embrace of God.

- Each of us is powerful beyond measure. I ask for guidance to make manifest this divinity I hold within to the grandest glory I can express.

- With God anything is possible. Within me this growing awareness is transforming my life in this pre-sent moment.

- I am ready to embrace my higher self and allow my life to be divinely guided.

- My connection to all is growing. As I grow and feel this connection to God and all that is, my higher self's purpose is shown and becomes a part of my life, moment to moment.

Our true purpose is to live a joyful life, using our feelings as our guide, and JOY the expression of who we truly are.

Remembering our True Selves

Re-membrance is putting back together, to re-join a part to the whole from which it comes. Each of us is part of the whole which some of us call God.

Re-membrance of our true being begins with acceptance of who we are right now. If a part of our life is not working, change is necessary. When our feelings tell us we are not happy, it is not an indictment, but an invitation to realize that we can be more than what we are allowing ourselves to be. Our "negative" feelings give us an opportunity to transform with love, a part of ourselves that does not fit our current image of who we are. Our feelings are one of the ways our spirit communicates with us.

When we act in a manner inconsistent with our spirit, we judge ourselves as bad and dish out the punishment we think such an action deserves. The judgment and subsequent punishment is what creates and prolongs mental and emotional pain in our lives. Our actions provide us with information to chart a new course, a more fulfilling one if we are willing.

We are not at the mercy of our experiences. We create them, and because they are our creation we can change them. However as long as judgment (I am right, you are wrong) exists, change cannot take place. When we release judgment and use love as our guide, our lives will unfold in new, more joyful ways. For as long as we hold onto our judgments without compassion, we cannot experience the joy which is possible in that situation.

So embrace love, first for self then for others. Observe that when we change how we perceive our experiences, how we feel about our experiences magically changes. It isn't our experiences that have changed, only our perspective.

Things happen, that's life. How we perceive it is an indication of how much of our divinity and true selves we allow to guide our every-moment experience of life.

When we share our feelings, we share our light.

Feelings: The Voice of our Spirit

When we suppress our feelings, we deny ourselves and the world (i.e. our world) the magnificence of who we are.

Our feelings are to be expressed, not suppressed. Telling someone how we feel is not a bad thing, its very expression is how we share our light. Whether the other person responds positively or negatively is not important. Our sharing should not be meant to elicit a response but merely as an expression of who we are.

If at any moment we do not like how we are presenting ourselves we have the power to change. But that choice is ours to make, and no one else's. No one can truly know the intention of our spirit or our life's purpose.

Responses from others do not have to be real for us. We can accept and recognize them as an expression of who they believe themselves to be. Their expression is based on their own life experiences, and cannot be true for us unless we believe they know more about us than we do, and therefore are more powerful than we are.

We are all beautiful and one way we express beauty is by being joyful. Joy is our natural state of being. True joy comes from accepting ourselves fully, including the parts of ourselves we judge to be bad or lacking in some manner.

We are born whole. Our challenge is in remembering our completeness, not in fleeting moments but in each and every moment of our lives. This is where our spirit can guide us, if we would allow it.

Our spirit is constantly expressing itself, guiding us to seeing the divine within ourselves. When we feel disconnected to our spirit we try different ways of reconnecting. When we search outside of ourselves, we may find momentary happiness, but we will eventually realize that what is outside of us cannot bring us true joy.

We may try drugs and alcohol but they cannot work. In fact no addiction can bring us to who we already are. It's like trying to catch the wind. We know it is there, we can feel it, but the physical act of trying doesn't work. So it is with our spirit's guidance; it must be felt and experienced, not controlled.

Remembering our true being begins with acceptance of who we are right now.

The Illusion of Fear

We've been brought up in a world with rules based on fear. Fear is the most effective tool used to get us to accept the ideas of others as our guide in how we should live. Fear creates illusions because it works in our imagination. We create life based on what we perceive as reality.

We are divine beings and any contrary belief is an illusion.

One of the major illusions we live by is that we are separate from each other; therefore it is okay to treat each other badly, without respect and even kill each other.

But you and I are one.

Whatever we do to others we first do to ourselves, and while its effects may not be physical it is just as real. Carrying out the act of hurting someone adversely affects everyone involved.

We are separate from no one and no thing, for the observer and the observed are connected and even changed by the observation. Our lives are affected by every experience.

Life is a testament to our beliefs, our beliefs affect our thoughts, and our thoughts determine our actions. Being aware of our connectedness is a life affirming, liberating force we can introduce into our lives. We can do this if we approach each interaction with others holding the thought, "I will not do or say anything that could cause others to feel worse about themselves."

Fear creates a feeling of separation and isolation, which is why we may feel lost. We can only feel lost by believing the illusion that we are separate from life.

Think of the most difficult person in your life. Part of the difficulty is you are both seeing the same thing quite differently. You may even be thinking he or she is crazy. If you are, I am sure the other person is thinking the same about you.

Near Hwy. #1 - Dryden, Ontario

Life's illusions end when we know we are already complete.

We are already all we need to be. We are part of 'All that is', and if we look closely enough, we will see that within us lies all the answers and the power needed to create our own life experiences.

With power comes responsibility, and our responsibility is to use our power to create our own life experiences helping ourselves and helping others without trying to control their lives.

To transcend any suffering we may feel, we must realize that pain is temporary but suffering can be long lasting, unless we release the illusions that can cause us pain. Illusions are created by the conclusions we make from experiences where we feel separated from our own divine nature.

We can end our illusions by bringing mindfulness into our lives. Mindfulness is the ultimate tool for creating awareness. Being mindful of the choices we make gives us the power to create a new reality, one based on awareness of our divine connection to each other and life.

Being mindful of how we feel, amplifies our spirit's voice, which I believe speaks to us through our feelings. When we can allow this divine energy to guide us, our ability to create is enhanced and gives us the confidence in ourselves to create and experience life in new, unlimited ways.

Rather than being jealous, applaud the accomplishments of others. The accomplishments of others can help us see life in a way we previously have not.

Know we are already complete through being alive, and as divine beings we have the power to create whatever we can imagine.

Trust

Trust is letting go of the need to control all aspects of our lives and letting God take care of the details. But how do we let go and still be responsible for the experiences in our lives? How can we have a desire or intention yet still remain unattached to the outcome?

We do this through giving up control of the process. Our responsibility is to desire an outcome but not to try and control the process.

Comparing our lives to others keeps us attached to the illusion of separation. When we compare ourselves to others we will usually find someone who has more than we do, or seems better off than we are. Yet this is living mainly from our ego. Our ego needs gratification; our spirit doesn't. Our ego has a purpose, but its purpose is not to be our master.

Feelings or thoughts of lack and failure are illusions, and their purpose is to help us recognize we are more than we've allowed ourselves to be. Yet even the idea of more is still of the ego but at a different level of being.

Some traditions believe that before we can be enlightened we must eliminate the ego. (This is assuming we want to be enlightened). Yet if the search for enlightenment means to become a more spiritual person, then becoming more of anything is still part of the ego. (I view enlightenment as a process of becoming aware of our connection to life through seeing the light within ourselves and each other. Through this light we do not "see others" but see everything as connections forming One).

Enlightenment helps us to be aware of all life's possibilities. Everything can serve a positive purpose, even our ego. But to live a balanced life, our ego must not be given more power than our spirit.

There is no training manual for life; we learn from experience. The awareness we bring to our experiences determines the quality of our lives.

The beauty of life is that we create it regardless of our level of enlightenment or conscious awareness.

Trust is desiring an outcome while giving up control of the process.

Exchange District, Winnipeg

*Thinking that we are separate from each other
is one of the biggest illusions in life.*

Each experience we create reveals life's big challenge. It is a challenge to walk on this tightrope where we know we are whole yet still desire to experience more of who we already are. This can only be done by creating illusions. We create the illusion of who we are not – so we can consciously create the reality of who we are.

Our higher self, our spirit, only desires to experience, nothing more, nothing less. We are a bundle of energy that is here to experience life and to do so from our highest idea of who we are or can be. Yet if our higher selves are complete, our true goal is recognizing and allowing the experiences in our lives to unfold without judgment. We then become an observer of the experience, and in doing so release attachment to a particular result. We allow all possibilities to be open to us as we experience life in each moment of now.

Life is a combination of experiences we create to help us remember our true selves, through being aware of our divine nature. Regardless of what we do, we are all becoming aware of our divinity and nothing we do changes that. For some of us awareness comes more slowly the stronger we hold onto the illusion that we are less than divine beings.

How do we develop trust?

Through developing awareness of our spirit and letting it help guide us, we realize there is nothing to fear, even death. Our spirit is our connection to our higher power, and this connection lets us know that our experiences support us even if we cannot see it in that moment.

As our awareness of our spirit grows, we continually develop more inner strength and increased acceptance of our own divine nature.

Trust cannot be given to us; it just is.

Trust is knowing that the answers we seek are within us, and the universe we see is our universe. Our experiences are the building blocks and formation of our universe; we each create our own. Yet the beauty of life lies in that while we each create our own experiences, life connects them all together.

Uni=one, verse=song therefore Universe = One Song.

We are single beings playing our own song, creating the whole we call "our universe." We are like a symphony with individual musicians playing their parts, contributing to the beauty of the whole. Each role is important regardless of how small a part we may think we play. We must each play our own part and attempting to play someone else's part creates a situation which robs the whole of our own-song, our contribution to the symphony of life.

Muriel Lake, Ontario

*"All that is" has to support us completely to
continue to be "All that is".*

Each of us experiences life in our own way, contributing our time, talents and abilities to help create a new and expanded universe. But the life we know now is different from our life of tomorrow. Our universe continually changes, and unless we change with it, we restrict our contribution, and the whole loses. Part of our responsibility is to create the highest expression of life we can imagine.

Knowing we are important to the whole allows us the freedom to create and appreciate our creation, and if we are not happy, to re-create it. Our awesome power to create is supported by all the other parts because each must create for the whole to continue to expand, and the universe must continually expand to continue to exist. This is the only trusting there is, that only our existence is necessary and no one part is more important than any other.

The energy of creation exists in us all, and we have the power to create anything we can imagine. As we become more aware of our creative ability, we create a new life because we accept a wider range of possibilities. Unless we can accept new possibilities we will continue to receive more of what we've already experienced, and this is okay if we are happy with our creation.

Trust allows the immense power some of us call God, "All That Is, divine energy, light, life, higher power (and more), to help co-create the experiences we imagine. Imagination is important because it expands our awareness beyond our current perceived limitations.

Trust is knowing who we are cannot be damaged or diminished by anyone unless we allow it, and regardless of how difficult our experiences, there is always a new day – unless there is not.

We know even in death, life is reborn – and the death of old beliefs and ways of thinking transforms us. That is the best life we can live, one where the ultimate outcome is never in doubt.

Know that the whole has to support us so we can continue to use our power and strength to create life. We are not at the mercy of life, because life has no preferences, it just is.

Life has to support us to continue to exist as life. Without support, life would be like a king without a kingdom. Both the king and the kingdom have power, and need the support of the other to exist. That is the true meaning and power of TRUST.

*All that occurs is a formation of the
divine experience of life.*

We Are God's In formation

We're told we cannot see God, maybe feel, but never physically touch "him." This idea is limiting because it says there is something God is not. If God created everything that exists, there is no thing that is not God.

To experience God we must go deep within ourselves. The conclusions we've made that we call reality act like layers over our core. Our core is where we find our essence and our connection to God or Universal Energy. It is the reality of who we are. What is not in harmony with this essence is an illusion. But the illusion must exist because to know God we must first know what is not God. And the only way to know what is not God is to create an illusion because there is no thing God is not.

This journey to knowing grows out of our frustrations about our life experiences. We know when something is not right, and if motivated enough we create change. We say to ourselves "My life is not working for my highest good; it has to change."

As we've created the idea of a devil to fill the space we feel God is not, so too we sometimes act in ways and think of ourselves in a manner inconsistent with who we truly are.

We are God's information

By allowing ourselves to act how we think God would act, we can begin to experience the light which encompasses all of our being. In each experience as we see ourselves as a part of God, we also see the people in our lives creating, and experiencing life as God in another form.

When there is disharmony in our lives we try to avoid the bad feelings they create. But who is feeling bad? And who creates the bad feelings?

Avoiding some feelings blocks us from embracing our experiences as opportunities to allow our true essence to manifest itself. Avoidance keeps us focused on our difficulties and what we do not have in our lives, and by focusing on our difficulties we create more of what we do not wish to experience. What we resist will and does persist in our lives.

We are always creating.

We may think others are causing our difficulties, but they are on their own path of creation. How we feel about another person's actions is based on how much we believe in our own power. Another person cannot cause us to act in a certain way. We choose how to respond to any action based on our thoughts and beliefs about ourselves and the experience.

The ability to choose is the most magnificent tool we've been given; it is the tool of creation. Even when we believe we do not have a choice and allow life to make choices for us we are exercising our free will. Not making a decision is a decision.

We must listen for the voice of our divine essence, which we first experience as a feeling. Our feelings can guide us in ways we cannot even imagine to a life of wonder and joy in each and every moment, if we allow it. Joy is part our true being, and when we do not feel joy, our thinking is focused on our being less than who we truly are.

We are God's in formation, and even a small acceptance of this brings with it the confidence there is nothing we cannot do, nothing we cannot have, and nothing we cannot be. This knowing gives us the power to create anything we desire.

Be aware of the awesome power you have in each moment, intend the best, and witness the formation of your experiences in alignment with your intention. Know that as Gods in formation, life has no choice but to align itself with your intention and create what you desire from the thoughts you hold most dear.

Joy is part of our true being.

Assiniboine Park Bridge, Winnipeg, MB.

Inner Peace ....

Living in your Light

Inner peace is felt when we are connected to the source of life within us. Our thoughts, beliefs, and feelings work together to direct the energy we use to create our reality.

We can only create in the present; living in the past diminishes our energy. In this pre-sent moment, past, present, and future comes together. This moment exists in the form determined by our previous choices and can only be lived fully by embracing the power that exists NOW.

Mindfulness (being completely aware in this moment) gives us the power to feel at peace. It allows us to go beyond the illusions we create in the present when we live in the past and/or worry about the future. Our illusions are like blinders that keep us unaware of the myriad of possibilities we have to create life in this moment of NOW.

We experience Inner Peace when we can accept life as it presents itself.

Whiteshell Provincial Park, Manitoba

Through accepting change and recognizing its purpose we become free.

Accepting Change

Why do we find change so difficult, when everything in life changes?

Our physical self is constantly changing. It is widely known there are no cells in our bodies which existed seven years ago. That means over one hundred trillion cells have entered and left our bodies. Our physical bodies are constantly changing yet we are still resistant to change.

Cocaine addicts experience their best high the first time they use; addiction comes from constantly trying to experience the same high. But they cannot, so they try more and more, thinking that more will recreate the exhilaration of the first high. Why is it so difficult to achieve the same feeling of the first high? Change. Their bodies change and although the drug may remain the same, the body's reaction does not. But this is who we are; we are changed with each experience.

Everything we experience contains within it the ability to help us expand our sense of who we are. The conclusions we make about our experiences determine whether we experience positive or negative feelings. However most of us, like the drug addict, experience something pleasant (like the love of another person), and we want more of the same feeling (because it feels so good to be loved). So instead of using the love of another to remember and expand the love within us, we try to hold onto what or whom we think is responsible for our feeling of love.

However, the stimulus that creates the good feeling within us is an illusion because it is outside of ourselves. For a brief moment someone joined us on our journey, and in that moment we felt a strong connection and were drawn to each other. Then, because we feel they were responsible for the happiness we feel, we give away our power by saying, "Here, you must continue to do the following to keep me feeling happy."

Yet, someone else's happiness is too burdensome a load and sooner or later that person will resent being responsible for our happiness. Then the search for happiness becomes a nightmare, and even this is acceptable, because like the addict, we remember the euphoria of the first high. We would sooner accept the illusion of never ending love than look at the truth, and remember we are responsible for our own feelings of love, joy, and happiness.

Everything changes and even if a relationship doesn't last, it doesn't mean that it did not work. If we can accept change in our relationships without drama, we realize there is a gift in every human experience if we take the time to look for it. In doing so, we realize we do not have to feel alone or diminished, because through the presence of our spirit we are connected to all that is, and love is the guiding light of that connection.

Tucson, Arizona

Grow in grace and find union with that divine presence through love.

Accepting Truth

The truth shall set us free, but each of us has our own truth.

Truth, not used as a way of getting what we want or to justify our actions, but the truth of who we truly are will set us free. Each of us has our own truth and living in harmony means accepting that the people in our lives have their own truth that is as important and real to them as ours is for us.

We are all born with the power to create any life we can imagine, and we expand life through our creations. We are not meant to create another person's existence because that is abuse (bad-use) of our power. We do this when we try to convince others that we know what is best for them.

All our experiences are part of our own divine plan. We all desire a fulfilling life, and this is what life wants for us. And if life wants what is magnificently beautiful for us, why should we accept any less for ourselves?

What we choose to create transforms us and can only affect others to the extent they allow it, as part of their own existence. We positively co-create with others when we do so by invitation. The energy of co-creating with others is far more powerful than the sum of our individual creations.

We are attracted to others who are in the same vibrational energy as we are. If our foundation for creating is fear, we will attract others sending out the same vibrational frequency. Similarly if our vibration is love we will attract others vibrating with the energy of love.

Our spirit provides the energy; WE determine how to use that energy, through love or fear. This is why our feelings help form the most important creative power we have. We act based on how we feel, and our feelings are part of how our spirit communicates with us.

Hwy. #1, near Thunder Bay, Ontario

*Change happens in an instant,
it is resistance to change that takes time.*

Our spirit is trying to guide us. If we are in a situation which feels "bad," our spirit is sending us a message that we are not in alignment with the part of us which is connected to Universal Energy/God. Its gift is awareness; it awakens us. We can then take whatever action is necessary to make a change to something that feels good.

Fear restricts and blinds us from being aware of the possibilities that exist in each moment. Fear lives in the present through regret about the past and concern for the future. It is extremely difficult to feel fear when our awareness is in the present moment, which is where creation takes place. Our power to create life exists in the present moment. We can learn from the past and plan for the future, but can only create in the present.

"The past is already gone, the future is not yet here. There's only one moment for you to live, and that is the present moment." Gautama Buddha

The present is a gift, and best of all we do not have to do anything to receive it. It is there for all of us, but we must accept it and use it in each moment for that is the most effective use of our creative power.

The universe is always changing, as are we. As part of All That Is, the moment we accept change we experience the immediate transformation of our lives.

Change is meant to bring us continually closer to fully accepting the spark of the divine that exists within us to help guide us to manifesting our most cherished reality. Accepting the truth of our ability to create awakens the unlimited power within to create a life of joy and love.

Change happens in an instant, it is resistance to change that causes pain and suffering.

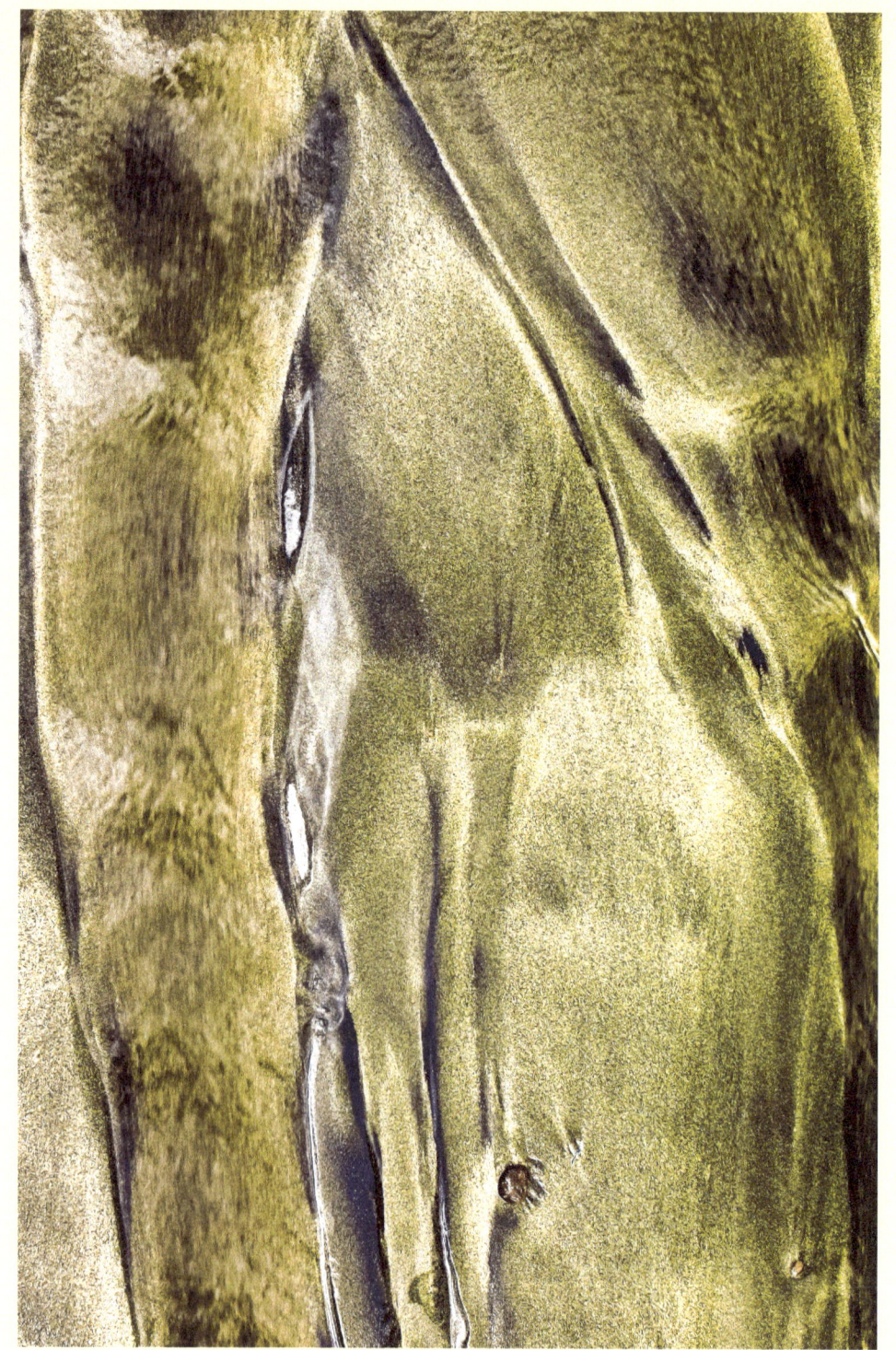

Awareness

Awareness is recognizing how we feel in each moment. Our level of awareness, and acknowledgment of our feelings indicate the ease with which we are using our energy in the present moment to create life.

Dis-ease shows us how our present beliefs are negatively affecting our lives.

Our most consistent thoughts create our beliefs. Our beliefs are the foundation for our lives, because they support the thoughts we have about ourselves. Beliefs, thoughts and feelings are interconnected and each affect the other.

Our beliefs are formed through the thoughts we have about an experience and the depth of those beliefs are determined by the amount of emotional energy we give that experience.

The stronger a belief is, the stronger our emotional attachment.

Our spirit is our connection to everything that has ever existed, is currently existing and will ever exist; it is not constrained by time. When our spirit's knowing and our human beliefs are not in alignment we think and act in ways that create dis-ease within us. My own belief is that:

Mental disease is mind dis-ease.

Physical disease is body dis-ease.

Emotional disease is spirit dis-ease.

To heal our lives we must become aware of the beliefs that create the need for healing in the first place. Observing how we feel develops awareness of how our beliefs are impacting our lives, and can be one of the best things we do for ourselves. Observing without judgment is a gift and a challenge because it may feel like we must use constant vigilance against our negative thoughts.

Awareness is the key to unlocking the door to a harmonious life.

When we judge ourselves harshly, we have no choice but to respond with what we consider an appropriate action. We become our own judge, jury and executioner. Gentleness and love for ourselves allows us to experience a level of perception that can create dynamic relationships, beginning with ourselves and then with others.

Awareness is an important part of physical, emotional and spiritual well being. Awareness grows out of mindfulness. Mindfulness is a practice we can develop to help us become more aware of our present moment experience, and the conclusion we make about that experience. It fosters an existence that allows us to live in this present moment.

Underlying all discomfort is a belief that is not serving our highest good.

Dis-ease is formed based on illusions we've allowed to become our reality. They indicate the false conclusions we've made about ourselves and our personal power.

Being aware is knowing that each experience contains within it the most perfect occurrence for us in this particular moment. With this level of awareness we develop confidence in our ability to handle whatever life presents.

Awareness reminds us that life unfolds as it must, and how we feel about an experience is a reflection of our most dominant thoughts and beliefs in that moment.

We are sometimes impatient for an experience to end, not realizing that unless we glean the understanding it brings, we will repeat the same or similar experiences until we grasp its meaning and purpose.

Patience: all will come in its time.

Our outer experiences are manifestations of our inner thoughts and deeply held beliefs. Pain's gift is awareness, and if we stop long enough to acknowledge our pain, we have given ourselves a gift that can and will transform our lives.

Alternately, love's gift reminds us of the capacity we have within to connect with others with respect and reverence for each of our individual journeys through life.

We are capable of accomplishing anything unless we believe we are not.

Muriel Lake, Ontario

Our experiences are a reflection of our most dominant thoughts.

Believing in Myself

Who I am is manifested in my life as my experiences, and is based on my thoughts of who I believe myself to be.

My image of myself determines my existence, and my experiences will confirm and reflect that image.

All possibilities exist now. In a world where all possibilities exist, my experiences are determined by what I expect, based on my beliefs. My beliefs effectively narrow the field of pure potential, coalescing into what I call my reality.

So how do I make changes in my life when I am not content with my current creations? The best and most lasting way I've found is to change what I believe about myself and my capabilities, through being mindful of how I feel in the present.

The most challenging situations in our lives come from disharmony in our interactions with others. If our childhood home life was loving then love is what we tend to create in our relationships. But when our early lives have been filled with conflict, we may unconsciously create conflict because that is what is familiar to us.

For example, we have distinct thoughts of who we think our parents are, and while these thoughts have some influence in our dating lives, it isn't until we are in a committed relationship or get married that these influences become much stronger.

The most important question I asked myself after separating from my ex-wife was, "Which one of my parents did I marry?" The answer was my father and this realization allowed me to better understand our relationship and see the quality of my choice of partner from a higher perspective. I knew neither one of us was at fault with the conflicts we created. We each had our own inner demons and failing to accept responsibility for our part only prolonged the pain we believed was caused by the other.

We were each doing the best we could, but the limitations we brought with us only created barriers to transcending the problems we faced together.

Clear Lake, Manitoba

The most challenging situations in our lives come from disharmony in our interactions with others.

Few of us are so knowledgeable that we know it all. If we believe we do, then this belief can be one of the major causes of the difficulties we face.

How can we make changes when our experiences are different than what we desire? By using our imagination. We can imagine a different way of being and using this as a guide, make changes which reflect who we would like to be. However before any of this can be achieved, we must be aware of how we feel.

Life is experience. Being aware of how we feel about our experiences can guide us to the areas that are not in harmony with our divine nature.

Our lives are not meant to be filled with conflict, and a peaceful existence is possible when we change our perception and awareness. Awareness helps us know what to change, and perception is the key which unlocks the door to change. Conflicts are internal and merely a manifestation of our limited thoughts and beliefs about ourselves and our experiences.

Anything we focus on, positive or negative, will be manifested in our lives using the energy of pure potential available to us all.

The athlete that accomplishes a new personal best trained their bodies and minds, and when both were in harmony a new level was attained. Until Dr. Roger Bannister broke the four-minute mile, everyone believed it was impossible. Dr. Bannister was convinced that slow and steady training would enable him to break the record. After breaking the "unbreakable record," within a month Australian runner John Landy broke Dr. Bannister's new unbreakable record, because the limited belief that it was impossible had changed.

I experienced this personally when I worked as a painter for a farm equipment manufacturer. My fellow painter and I were Bruce Lee fans and would often discuss the amazing feats he'd accomplished. One of these was his ability to do pushups on his thumbs only. I had practiced doing pushups using my fingertips, but thumbs only was a stretch. He bet me 25 cents I couldn't do it, and three times I tried and failed.

Finally I decided that to accomplish something I'd never done before I would have to go beyond my currently held beliefs. I changed my self-talk and for the next half hour told myself that Bruce Lee was a man and if he could do it so could I. I repeated the mantra "if he could do it I can do it,"

Anything we focus on and put energy into will be enhanced to the highest ideal we can imagine.

When I felt I was ready, I told my friend that I was going to DO it, not try. I got down on the floor and very carefully did my first ever thumbs pushup. After doing it once, and now armed with the knowledge that it was part of my experience, I did five more without stopping. Years later without practicing I could still do them, and the only significant change was my self-talk.

That experience taught me that anything I want to change in my life must first begin with changing my thoughts and beliefs about my ability to create it.

If we were to examine our lives, we would remember instances when we were able to accomplish something we may not have first thought possible. However, if our image of ourselves is based on the illusion that we are not capable of doing what we imagine, we limit our experience. If we can imagine it we can accomplish it.

We sometimes tend to dismiss our accomplishments as coincidence and chance, and rob ourselves of the transformative power contained in the experience. The power to create change is in each one of us and it is important to use this power as fully as we can because our highest achievements are part of our contribution to the expansion of life.

We are all capable of great things unless we think we are not. We grow from stretching ourselves and doing something we haven't done before or failed to accomplish in the past.

If for a moment we would see the divine beings we are and accept this as our reality, the joyous life we seek would stop being a pipe dream and manifest itself in each and every moment, regardless of the circumstance.

It is then that even the so-called negative that happens in our lives would not be a reason to stop creating. Our negative experiences challenge us to declare to the world, "I have within me all the tools I need to create a beautiful life." This is our right by birth. When we believe we are capable, we become aware of the many possibilities available for us to create whatever we can imagine.

Believing in ourselves is ultimately a declaration of our acceptance of our divinity and the energy within to create our own life experiences, with love.

Elkhorn, Manitoba

Setting clear boundaries is an act of Self Love.

Self Confidence

Why is it so difficult for some of us to achieve and maintain confidence in ourselves?

We live in a world dominated by fear. We're taught to control what we fear, believing that control is how we can eliminate its effect in our lives. Control gives us a feeling of power. Yet at the first indication of loss of control we lose this feeling of power.

Developing confidence in ourselves can be fleeting and fragile, yet when achieved, our lives are enriched in so many ways.

Because of our familiarity with fear, most of us more easily accept negative comments about ourselves than positive ones.

How can we develop the inner strength to maintain a strong sense of who we are?

Early influences at a time when we are still forming our place in the world greatly affect how we feel about ourselves and ultimately who we grow up to be.

In my teens I began a quest to understand how my thoughts and beliefs limit my life experiences. My first challenge was understanding how my shyness was affecting the quality of my life. The book Psycho-Cybernetics by Dr. Maxwell Maltz, was the first to teach me that our beliefs create our reality.

One lesson I learned from my father was that I would never amount to anything. He repeated it enough times that after awhile I didn't need his input to continue to reject myself and my accomplishments. As an adult I realized I was still unconsciously continuing his programming.

Even today, long after I'd first become aware of its negative impact, I still need to be vigilant in being aware of when this belief affects my thoughts and actions. It is a part of me, and denying its existence gives it the power to work in me unconsciously.

Words matter.

The hurtful words of others can deeply impact our psyche, maintaining a presence in our lives long after they should. It is our acceptance of hurtful words as fact that gives it the power to continue to negatively impact our lives.

Sturgeon Creek, Winnipeg

*Each time we do something in spite of our fears we enhance
our confidence, regardless of the outcome.*

Changing and transforming the power we give to negativity requires acceptance of its presence as part of what we believe about ourselves. Only then can we regain the power to transform them.

If we approach our growth as eliminating all the negative within us, we can and will continue to find something to feel bad about. We will feel moments of joy and even bliss but the words of another, a smell, a touch, a song, can all trigger a negative reaction within us.

When we can accept the parts of ourselves we do not like, we give ourselves the power to create ourselves anew. We are a combination of lightness and darkness.

Fear of our darkness can keep us from realizing that when we accept our darkness as part of us and still love ourselves, a new understanding develops which allows us to tap into the peace that exists within.

I have found that living confidently occurs when I am aware of my limitations but focus and act from my strengths.

Confidence gives me the courage to take risks, acting responsibly, while embracing the unknown as part of the process. I can then recognize challenges as part of my creation to help me fully develop my life story.

How do I recognize confidence in action? Through:

- Knowing I do not need to fear making mistakes; mistakes are a part of life.
- Admitting my mistakes regardless of the consequences.
- Acknowledging and recognizing the accomplishments of others.
- Standing up for my beliefs, even when they are not the most popular.
- Being able to accept the praise of others without actively seeking it out.
- Accepting myself and others the way we are.
- Demonstrating love for myself and others.

Confidence is a divine tool that allows me to act from a position of strength, not because I am better than others, but because I know there is no "other." We are all co-creating life using the gifts we have, and my part is to embrace life with all my beingness. I help expand life by fully utilizing my gifts, thereby contributing to the continued expansion of life.

Canola Field, Manitoba

All that you can imagine is a possibility for you.

Imagine Life into Being

What do you need in life? Nothing. There is nothing you need to make your life complete. If there was you wouldn't exist.

Life is complete and you are life.

When you need something, you give your power to it. If you need the love of another, you give your power away to them.

If you need money, you give your power away to money, and because it is in the hands of others, you give your power away to them. It could a job, a thing or a person. Regardless of the need, the end result is that need creates subservience, which means that someone else controls how you feel and live.

When you intend to experience life in a particular manner, and that intention is strong, you activate the power within to help create your intention.

Needs are what we feel we cannot live without, while desire is an intense feeling that comes from earnestly wishing for something without feeling we have to have it, knowing we will experience it, eventually (my definition).

All you can imagine is a possibility for you. Imagination is the starting point of creation. It attracts energy, which begins to form into the manifestation of what you imagine. It is like a ship leaving port. No one can see the final destination but through constantly adjusting its course, the ship will eventually reach its destination.

Reclaim the power you have given away, because you are meant to use that power to create the life you imagine. The more you give away by doubting yourself, means you have that much less to manifest your desires.

How do you feel about the world you've created? If you do not feel GOOD about the world you've created, lighten up and recreate it.

Your awareness is your world. Make the changes that would look like, sound like and feel like the world you would like to live in. Your awareness and beliefs about life are your reality, and without you life cannot and does not exist.

Consider life as a colouring book. We are each given the opportunity to colour it however we choose to create the canvas called "My Life."

It's your world and you are the creator of it.

Twin Towers - World Trade Centre, New York

The Power of Fear

What is the power fear has in our lives?

Fear can rob us of our dreams. It can kill any initiative we may have to accomplishing something worthwhile and in doing so, fear robs the world of our contribution. Fear stops us in our tracks.

Collectively fear can rob us of our freedom.

The result of the war on terror has created what the terrorists intended. The purpose of terror is to create fear. The US has been called the land of the free, yet most Americans have given up a certain measure of freedom to feel safer from the terrorists.

The war on terror has changed the way we view others and ultimately the way we live. It's affected our economy and no one has been immune to its effects. Personally, I had a cousin and her boyfriend who both died in the attack on the World Trade Centre buildings on September 11, 2001 in New York City. The graphic and constant news coverage that played out in front of us made the fear seem more real for many of us.

But what is fear? Is it real? What is real for us is what we say reality is. Fear can be used by those in power to limit our personal rights and freedoms. On a personal level, fear can limit our power, but our true selves are unlimited. If we were to know who we truly are, we would fear nothing, as we are divine beings with the power to create anything we desire.

Everything that exists is energy. Fear is one way we choose to use our energy when we doubt ourselves. When we feel fear, we are like a deer frozen in the headlights of an oncoming vehicle. It immobilizes us.

How can we change what we fear?

In a spiritual sense eliminating fear means shining light on our fears, which brings them out of the dark. Fear is like a terrorist who can only achieve their goals by keeping invisible until they create destruction in our lives. We can only change our fears by recognizing them and creating a plan to transform them.

We must be willing to look at the positive intention behind our fears. There is something positive behind all that occurs in our lives. As an example, we may be afraid of heights because we know if we fall, we can die. Similarly a fear of snakes may protect us from being poisoned. However, we can go overboard with our fears.

To understand our fears we may ask, "Is this a rational fear or is it irrational? Do I react without awareness and allow my fears to rule my life?" By taking the time to look at our fears openly without emotion, we give ourselves the power to transform them. This transformation releases the energy required to create life in a new way.

Petroforms, Whiteshell Provincial Park

Know your fears, embrace them, shine your light on them, for only then can you use the energy they require to create the wonderful, joyful life you are meant to live.

In the past I've had a fear of not having enough money. My response used to be keeping to myself, not doing the things I enjoy because I would need the money to pay bills. However when I sat down and looked at the money I had and laid everything out on paper I felt a sense of relief. I found I didn't have to worry, because I had enough but didn't know it. I brought my fear out in the open and that was the first step in transforming it.

Here is an exercise for a better understanding of fear. (Taken from Emissary of Light by James Twyman).

Take a moment and think of the most pleasant and joyful experience you've ever had. Become aware of where in your body that energy resides. Now release the thought of the experience and concentrate on the energy. Let it build until it feels like a force growing inside you. Take the energy and bring it into your heart and imagine a tiny door opening in your heart and let the energy out into the world.

Now think of a time when you felt intense fear. Become aware of where in your body that energy resides. Release the thought and emotion of the fear and experience and concentrate on the energy. Let it build (the energy – not the emotion) and move it into your heart, let it stay there for a moment and then imagine a tiny door opening and let the energy move out into the world.

The effect of this exercise is to realize that fear, love and any other emotion is energy. It is the thoughts we attach to the energy which creates the feeling of love or fear. When we can see our fears as energy we realize we have the power to direct that energy in any way we desire. Our fears have no energy or creative power by themselves, only what we give it.

Societal fears are the same. In Canada, a Member of Parliament (Congressman in the US) was forced to resign because after a visit to the Middle East, he said that Canada should change its policy of not communicating with terrorists. I personally did not understand what was wrong with that statement. He didn't say negotiate, just communicate.

Ultimately, sitting or talking face to face removes the power terrorists have. We've tried bombing and fighting them into submission, and all that's been accomplished is the creation of more terrorists. Unless we bring them into the light they will remain in the dark, which is where they have power.

Ultimately, we will realize that personally and collectively, we must be willing to view our fears in the light, openly and honestly. Only then can we transform them, because the power of fear exists in the dark recesses of our minds.

Know your fears, embrace them, shine your light on them – for only then can you release the power needed to create the wonderful, joyful life you are meant to live.

How Judgment Creates Conflict

In an effort to be spiritual do we have to be perfect? We carry with us an image of what a spiritual being is. We think of Jesus, Mohammed, Buddha, Krishna, Mother Theresa - and feel that we cannot be as "good" as they were.

We are all spiritual beings with a divine contribution to make using our unique gifts and talents. We each have our own contribution to make in life. What we choose should be a personal choice, not one derived from the judgments of others.

Where does the need to be perfect come from? We are all perfectly imperfect. Our feelings of imperfection come from the well-meaning judgment of others about how we should live and who we should be.

We carry perceived injustices like a badge of honour, and use this to colour our view of the world.

What we do to others, we first do to ourselves even if only in our imagination. To abuse another, we must first hold within ourselves the belief that abuse is a solution, and this belief affects us physically, mentally, emotionally, and spiritually. We may not realize that in doing so we create negative karma for ourselves.

Karma means "intentional action" and refers to the universal law of cause and effect. Karma is created not only by physical action but also by thoughts and words.

We are responsible for the outcome of our own words, thoughts and actions that affect another in any way. Accepting responsibility for our words, thoughts and actions allows us to live a more harmonious life.

Emotions of inadequacy, guilt and shame guide us to areas within ourselves where we do not accept the divine light within. These emotions are a part of us but they also represent our illusions, which we project into the world as our opinions. When our opinions differ from those of another, conflict can arise.

Some common illusions:

- For us to gain someone has to lose.
- What we desire in life is more important than what others may want.
- We are separate from each other.
- Life is hard.
- We can't trust anyone.
- Doing wrong is okay if no one knows.

Muriel Lake, Ontario

My experiences are a reflection of what is inside me.

We introduce conflict into our interactions with others when we choose to deny our illusions as a part of who we are. To transcend our illusions, we do not need to judge them, but to see them as an indication of beliefs that are not serving our higher good. They are not wrong or right, they are simply a tool for growth.

Wrong is a judgment we place on an experience – and no experience is wrong, it just is.

We must embrace ourselves and know that the divine light within can illuminate our path if we trust it.

To transform our judgments about an experience, we need to know that if we are willing to trust, the God within will guide us.

It is sometimes difficult to recognize the illusions we have about ourselves. This is where our connection to those we love can help us.

If we are open and aware, the friend we talk to, the people we trust, can slow us down enough to help us see the truth of our situation. That is the value others can have in our lives. Embrace them, if not physically then mentally, and thank them for being a guide, a part of the divine which loves us enough to tell us the truth of who we currently are.

So see them as angels, for they show us a mirror of ourselves. What we do with that guidance will show us how much we've remembered about who we truly are. Our acceptance and any positive action that follows can guide us to love and inner peace.

It is hard to live without judgments. Everything we decide is a conclusion we make based on judgment. Our challenges arise when we accept our judgment as reality not only for ourselves but also for the people in our lives.

So where do we look for answers when things in our lives are not how we wish them it to be? Are the answers outside of us or are they within?

The world we experience is our world. The people we meet are a reflection of who we see our self as being at that moment. Our experiences represent what is inside us. This is why something that bothered us yesterday may not bother us today. For today, as in each day, we are born anew. As we sleep each night, our beliefs about our experiences of the day are integrated overnight into who we are tomorrow.

Therefore it's important to be clear about how we see the events in our lives, and realize that judgment can hold us back from experiencing the divine presence within.

Let love be your guide and joy your expression of who you are.

Free Will

The ability to make a choice is the ability we use to create life. Creating life is the domain of Gods, which makes us God in the world in which we create.

Marianne Williamson from A Return to Love writes, "Our deepest fear is not that we are inadequate. Our deepest fear is that we are powerful beyond measure. It is our light not our darkness, that most frightens us."

This passage tells us we are more powerful than we've been told or accepted. The main questions to ask are, "If we have a choice to live in light or live in darkness, why does it seem like darkness is our first choice most of the time?" And, "Is our ability to choose the simple indicator of our power?"

Our ability to choose allows us to create based on our most dominant thoughts, ideas and beliefs at that moment. If we can see ourselves as loving, creative beings, our choices will be dramatically different than when we choose to see ourselves as limited beings.

When we accept our ability to create, we fulfill our right by birth to be magnificent creators of life if we so choose. Whatever we decide, and what we believe about ourselves will be the guiding light of our creations. We are always creating; our challenge is to imagine the best we desire, and use this as the starting point of our creations.

This ability and no other is what allows us the ability to be like God in our own present moment of creating life. Embrace the light within; it is the energy we use to create positive or negative outcomes. Choose wisely.

Be grateful and know there is no failure in life when we choose to live in-spirit, that is inspired.

My Gift

My gift to others is not to tell them my truth but to inspire them to find their own.

I do this by being quiet and listening when the people in my life express themselves. When I allow others to share of themselves and I listen intently, I create an opportunity to deeply connect with them.

Love is a great teacher. Love others enough to realize that within each human exchange exists an opportunity to connect with the oneness we all share. This does not mean we are the same, but we share the same divinity. Their search for meaning and purpose is divine in and of itself, and if I listen, I open a window to greater communication. When this happens we connect on a higher level.

When I meet people who tell me their truth about my experience, I feel diminished. It's as though I do not know my own path, and if I follow this "guidance," I lose myself.

Recognizing that "my life" is not for someone else to live, helps me realize that for any question I have, I also have the answer within.

Love others enough to help them realize that they are divine and already know the answers to their most pressing questions. One of the biggest challenges in life is knowing what I want. To achieve clarity I must know the correct questions to ask and trust that the right answers will arise from within.

What blocks us is not accepting our own divine nature. We need to recognize that the divine presence within only wants what's best for us, and the opportunity to express this goodness in our lives. When we doubt ourselves, we stop listening. We allow the business (busy-ness) of our lives to cloud the finest guide we will ever know, our feelings.

So, when we meet those who seek guidance or the answer to their life's challenges, help them realize that within them exists their greatest guide, their feelings. By asking, "How do you feel about that?", we can help guide them to the part of themselves that already knows the answer.

When we feel overwhelmed or unsure of what to do, we must trust our feelings. This is how our spirit speaks to us.

When we do not trust our feelings, we make decisions using only our rational mind. In using our rational minds we can only draw upon prior experiences, and therefore will only get more of what we already have.

To live an inspired life, our feelings must be a guide, a part of the divine that exists within for the soul-purpose of guiding us to our highest achievements and the fullest expression of who we are. It is here we find peace and in turn live our lives to the highest idea we have of ourselves, life, and God.

When we do this, truly successful living follows, as it must. This is God's gift to us and our gift to the world. Be grateful and know there is no failure in living when we live in-spirit – that is inspired.

Kakabeka Falls, Ontario

There is no common reality but an individual reality.

What is Reality?

Reality is an agreement we make with ourselves about our present circumstances based on perceptions learned from past experiences.

Reality is formed and influenced by the thoughts and ideas we've allowed to become our "truth."

These thoughts become beliefs we allow to control our present moment. They cannot help but be distorted because we affirm that our present experiences are the same as our past. What we must realize is, the present can only be lived and experienced. We cannot live joyfully and with inner peace with concerns of yesterday or worries about tomorrow.

Living in the past serves no positive purpose in the present as it exists only in our memory, distorted by conclusions we made at a time when we were not as experienced as we are today. The present can only be experienced now. The moment we talk about it or try to describe it, it's already the past.

Similarly the future has not yet happened, yet worrying about it sends a message that we do not have the ability or confidence to live with whatever happens. Thus we limit the wide range of experiences possible, not utilizing the full power of pure potential available to us all.

When we observe an experience, we may only see one possibility – yet away from our limited observation all possibilities exists. Therefore what we call reality is based on a personal observation influenced by our beliefs.

To fully experience our reality, we must choose to live with awareness of the power within each moment of now. Reality is happening; it is now, and we have the power to create it however we imagine.

Living in the past or future limits our ability to live a full and enriching life and contributes to diminishing our sense of self. Living in the present is knowing we are okay now and in each and every moment of our existence. Only in being open to all possibilities in each experience can we truly live. Mindfulness helps us be aware of the power available to us in the present moment.

The moment we declare something as real, we've narrowed the full range of possibilities to a view that identifies it as our declaration of reality. However, we must decide whether our choices will be based on the highest idea we have of ourselves or the limited view we have made about our prior experiences. If all possible realities exist for us, why choose any but the best we can imagine?

Black Rock, Tobago

The Dis-ease of Being Right

What is this need we have for being right? Given the choice, some people would prefer to be right, even if it means losing a relationship.

This is one of the most common ways we lose friendships and relationships.

We sometimes feel that to acknowledge we have made a mistake is a personal failing. We must be perfect. Religions cling to this based on "the righteousness of the Lord," yet even religions change their rules.

The most important part of our existence is our relation to each other. This is why those closest to us are called relatives and are familiar (families).

We do not enrich our power through being right but through the realization that common union (communion) with others is the greatest opportunity to express our true power, which is our love for ourselves and others.

The relationships closest to us are the ones which create the greatest conflict because we care about what our friends and families think about us. They also know how to push our buttons.

I believe we each do the best we can with the information we have at that moment, and as we acquire more information we make better decisions.

We do not have all the answers. Life is meant to provide us with answers to the difficulties we face through learning from our prior and present experiences. The level of awareness we develop will determine how many times we face the same type of challenges.

Relationships provide us with the greatest opportunities for growth and understanding of ourselves and the people in our lives. It is much easier to be centered and have inner peace when alone than in a relationship. We are attracted to the right person that can propel us to our next stage of growth if we face the challenges that come up with an open mind and open heart.

Right and wrong are judgments, and all judgments are based on illusion.

Cuthbert Grant's Mill, Winnipeg

We have the power to create in our world anyway we think is best for us.

Our true self is magnificent. But when we rely on another for our happiness we cannot see that. We give away our power. Deep inside we know that, but we feel we've invested so much of ourselves in our roles that we are reluctant to change. We will accept mistreatment from others as long as the pain of change feels greater than the pain of staying in a relationship that is no longer working for us.

When we choose to put our happiness in the hands of another, we in effect tell the other person, "You are in control of my life." This is when abuse and neglect can begin to surface, because the happiness of another is too big a burden to bear.

To ease our reliance on our need to be right, we must embrace our inner indestructible self. We need to know that who we are right now is okay and the other person is also okay. We will then realize there is no other person, but merely a mirror image of our current thoughts, ideas, feelings and beliefs.

Right and wrong are judgments, and judgments can be based on illusions. If we are connected to All That Is, then in judging another, we first judge ourselves. Any judgment we make that does not see the beauty in others, and in each and every experience is based on an illusion.

We have the power to create in our world anyway we think is best for us. Accepting the judgment of others can prevent us from finding and living our purpose. Our purpose is the fuel that provides the energy to live our lives with genuine intent, utilizing the creative power that exists within us all.

The Truth can Set us Free

Our mind constructs our freedoms and our prisons. When we are willing to look at the truth of any situation, we become free from the bondage and limitations that can be part of any experience.

When we feel someone is untruthful, we may hold onto the rightness of our position. Being stuck in a position limits our growth. We cannot move on until they acknowledge our truth.

What is truth?

Our beliefs about a situation are what we project as the truth. But regardless of how strongly we may feel, it is only our truth. The more strongly we feel we know the truth, the more attached we become to being right, and this is one of the main causes of conflict. To transcend possible conflict we must realize that the other person has his or her own truth that is as valid and right as ours.

Dealing with my ex-wife, I felt I "knew" the truth but found greater peace within myself when I realized it was only my truth and I did not need to be defined by it. By choosing to live in peace, and not be attached to being right gave me the power to direct my own life and not let circumstances or her thoughts, words and actions determine who I am or how I feel.

We are not victims. Thinking of ourselves in this manner allows a past situation to control our lives in the present. We are so much more.

All past experiences exist as memories. So how do we allow our memories to control us? When we let a memory determine our thoughts, actions, and belief about ourselves we give up our power to the past, and in allowing the past to determine our present we remain stuck, unable to define the direction of our lives.

Our divine self, the one we are connected to and which survives physical death, is connected to the energy of pure potential. Pure potential aligns universal energy and allows us to choose and create the life we desire.

Allowing the choices and opinions of others to hold us back is a travesty. Each of us is the single sperm that won the multi-million sperm race to be manifested as "me". After that, all else we face should be simple.

When we doubt ourselves, we allow the energy of fear to guide us. What we focus on expands, whether it is the energy of love or fear. Life has no preference. Life reflects the experiences which indicate how we are using the energy available to us all. Life is this joyful present that says we are magnificent, and all the powers in the universe have come together so we can be here NOW. This moment is the only creative time we have.

Assiniboine Park, Winnipeg

*We are each part of Universal energy
manifesting in different forms.*

So we can accept the truth that:

- No one can diminish us without our permission.
- We are the most magnificent creation ever, with a mind that makes a computer seem but a toy.
- We have a body which performs millions of functions in each moment to exist and does it all simultaneously.
- We have the ability to choose our response in each moment.
- We shape our future from our thoughts in this moment.
- As children of the Divine we are creative. With this awesome power, what do we choose to be responsible for?
- We can change our lives by changing our beliefs and ideas about ourselves. This is how we create meaningful change.
- Every experience occurs to remind us of our power. We choose how to respond.
- We experience true joy in helping others.
- We cannot give what we do not have. If we give joy and love, we will find more within.
- We are all one, and this is one of the biggest "truths" we can accept.

We are affected by everyone we meet, and part of our purpose is to create meaningful relations. Sometimes we feel alone even when in the company of others. But we are never alone. We have only to think of someone and some part of them is with us if only in thought. We can then use thought in a creative way to reduce loneliness.

We are born with an awesome power that never diminishes. It's the power to create. We are unique, powerful, creative beings that need only to accept that this is who we are. When we accept our power and live our purpose, life becomes harmonized with our inner being and we experience the symmetry and beauty which exists now in each moment.

Truth lives, right here – right now. At this moment we have all the power and all the answers we will ever need, WITHIN.

Mantario Trail, Manitoba

We do not have to defend our right to be.

We are All Magnificent

We do not have to defend our right to be. We do not have to make excuses for why we feel a certain way or feel bad for a thought or action. If we do not like a thought or action, simply stop. That is our choice and we do not have to defend it.

This is how we express our will in our lives. It is our will, not someone else's which guides us to joyous living.

Reclaim the power in your life by not defending yourself. We give away our power by defending ourselves to others. However, the biggest loss of power is when we defend ourselves to ourselves.

What we say has the power to create our magnificence or to make us feel inadequate, When we say "Why did I do that, I am so stupid sometimes," or "I should know better than that," we diminish ourselves. If we did know better, in that moment we would do better.

Each of us does the best we can in each moment with the information we have.

We each won the first and biggest race we will ever face in our lives. We beat out over one million other little racers to become the human being you see in the mirror each day. The person reflected back to you is magnificent just because you exist.

"If we do not go within we go without." We only feel inadequate when we compare ourselves to others.

Look inside; find what inspires you in each moment and in doing so you relax into your magnificence. Ease up on yourself and live the life of wonder you are here to live. This should be your first step to living your life on purpose. Reclaim your right to be, not for any reason other than because you're here, and I for one am glad.

Why am I Hurting?

We feel hurt usually through the actions of others. Having power over our own actions means we have the capacity to change what is not working.

The power to create meaningful change exists within each and every one of us. When someone does something that others say should hurt us, we give away our power if we accept this belief.

What others do defines them, not us. The decision to abuse another is a personal one. It thus follows that the outcome of their choices is also their responsibility, not ours.

Our response can be love, even in the face of abuse. We do not have to love the situation or action, only love ourselves. When we love ourselves enough to forgive others for their choices, we are not saying their actions are okay. We are saying we no longer choose to suffer by continuing to carry the pain their actions caused.

Loving ourself allows us to resist the impact of another person's choices in our lives. Our love has immense power, and we must allow its energy to move us in whatever way is appropriate to continue loving ourselves.

When we hurt ourselves we say "I hurt myself," separating the hurt from ourselves. When others hurt us we say, "I'm hurt," identifying with the pain we think we must feel. However it is important that when we feel the actions of others are meant to cause us pain, we separate ourselves from their actions. We can then say to ourselves, "They tried to hurt me but I refuse to accept their pain."

How? The solution comes easier when we do not attach our emotions to their actions. Whatever we are emotionally attached to, we give our power to. Some may say that our emotions define us, and that's true as emotions give us an experience of life. However, we choose what emotions we want to accept, those based on love or those based on fear. This is the foundation of personal power.

Choice, which by definition is free.

The power to create meaningful change exists within each and every one of us.

Assiniboine Park, Winnipeg

*We are magnificent beings creating life based on our
most deeply held thoughts and beliefs.*

Who am I?

I am God expressing itself as me. All that I need exists within. I co-create my life from my most dominant thoughts and beliefs using the all-powerful energy that formed the universe. I am supported by this energy and it is supported by me.

Our connection with the energy that created the universe and what materializes in our lives is the highest creation possible based on our thoughts and beliefs. When we recognize and use this power, we can create any life we can imagine. Not recognizing and accepting this power can show up in our lives as scarcity, lack, and feeling inferior.

When we compare ourselves to others we do ourselves a dis-service, because in doing so we tell ourselves that we do not trust our own power of creation. We are unique storehouses of energy that only needs to align our highest thoughts with the energy that creates life. As we allow this alignment, our intentions are manifested.

We are always creating, and if we think we can or we think we can't, the universe will validate our most dominant thoughts with proof.

We cannot joyfully create what others think we should because our spirit does not understand another person's intentions as a guiding force in our lives. When we allow others to direct our lives, we put shackles on our creativity. What we attempt to create is done with resistance, and resistance acts as a counter force to our creation.

Creating a magnificent life begins with awareness of our imagination and our dreams. In our dreams we create all that is needed to complete the dream. In our awakened state we can do the same, bounded only by the limitations we believe exists in our lives. Our dreams are a snapshot of our limitless capabilities. They act as a reminder of what we can accomplish when we allow the rational part of us to rest and not be the only force of creation in our lives.

We are always creating and if we think we can or we think we can't, the universe will validate with proof.

Can we allow this to happen in our wakened state? Yes. That is the purpose of remembrance. As we awaken, we are reminded that each moment is an opportunity to remember our limitless capabilities when we allow our true selves to guide us.

We are reminded of the magic which happens at birth. This tiny particle that we couldn't see if it was placed right in front of us contained within it who we are today. It had the building blocks of our physical selves. But this is only part of who we are. Another equally important part is the energy that connects us to All That Is.

This energy is our connection to each person we meet, each thought we possess, and each and every experience we have. It is the driver of the vehicle that is our body, the navigator of our life, and our use of it is determined by what we choose to experience.

Do we choose to live with the positive intention that anything we can imagine we can create? That within and around us miracles happen each and every moment of our existence?

With awareness comes the realization that we can be marvelous, magnificent beings who create our intentions according to our most fervently held beliefs and thoughts of ourselves.

So ask yourself, "Knowing this at this moment, how do I choose to live?"

Our feelings help create our experiences.

We Must Heal How we Feel

True healing beings with changing how we feel. When we continue to make the same choices we always have, we are choosing to continue to feel the same.

If we call an experience "bad" and continue to make the same choices, we are choosing to feel the same way over and over again.

When we temporarily remove self (who my ego says I am), we can then see the higher meaning in each experience. Ultimately it is our choice whether we move easily, creating experiences in harmony with our higher selves or creating from ego, resisting the learning inherent in each experience and thus create dis-harmony.

Harmony and conflict each has a purpose; it is how we feel that gives an experience its meaning and purpose in our lives.

We know we are in harmony when we feel good. When we feel good, we trust the goodness in life. This goodness helps us feel loving, and loving is easy when we are in harmony with life.

When we are in conflict, loving is more difficult, and so to protect ourselves we make love conditional.

Who is the 'self' we are protecting?

The only 'self' to protect is the self we think we are, our small self, our ego self. Our Higher Self does not need protection. One question we can ask ourselves is, "Are we putting so much energy into protecting our 'self' that we have precious little energy left to truly enjoy life?

Living requires energy, and our feelings determine how that energy is used. Our feelings affect our thoughts, which then strengthens our beliefs, which then creates an experience, which in turn creates stronger feelings. The cycle of feelings, thoughts and beliefs expands as long as we resist changing them when we feel they are not working for us. That is why we must heal how we feel.

This Insignificant Voice

I cry and no one hears,
 I shout but it comes out as a whisper,
 I sob silently, my energy is gone,
 I feel I am not heard.

But what of my ears?
 Do I listen or hear
 when someone is crying or shouting?

When my own voice is so loud
 or I feel my pain is so great,
 I cannot hear another.

So here we are all insignificant voices
 to anyone but ourselves.

I open my ears to all insignificant voices.
 I know it doesn't matter if mine is not heard.

If I listen, the voice of another
 falling softly, gently on my ears,
 will mirror my own truth screaming to be heard,
 and my voice will be insignificant no more.

Life
Experiencing the Divine in All

*L*ife is all that is. It's our combined experience of 'good' and 'bad' which forms the whole we call life.

Our experiences form the fabric of our lives, created through our most dominant thoughts and beliefs. What we concentrate on, and put our thoughts into, will be created in our lives.

What is most important is how we feel about our experiences. We tend to create or more accurately re-create our negative experiences when we avoid our feelings about them.

Life is about growth, learning, and remembering our divinity. And our most challenging creations are the ones we have with each other. When we communicate with others, what we feel is based on our beliefs about the other person, the situation, and most importantly ourselves.

When we act with confidence, we accept our ability to live the life we desire. Therefore we must allow the part of ourselves that knows we are divine beings living a human experience to guide our lives.

Regardless of the circumstance, we will see all that occurs as a process of life unfolding.

Every moment counts, if not try missing one.

We give a lot of power to fear, and the foundation of fear is doubt.

Allowing

Why is it such a challenge to trust and allow the energy of life more expression in our lives? Growing up in a world that preaches you'll believe it when you see it, makes it difficult to trust what we do not see. When our concept of ourselves is limited, we find it difficult to trust in that power to support us, without conditions.

Why do we find it so difficult to trust ourselves and our power to create? We've been taught that God gave us the power to make any choice we desire, yet religion teaches us that we still have to make the right choice. So we can make any choice as long as it pleases God. How can we trust a deity that gives us "conditional free will?"

This belief creates doubt and makes finding the strength to continue trusting in a higher power illusive. Sometimes when we think we've grown beyond a certain way of thinking, we experience a setback and doubt ourselves. Living consciously, with awareness of our creative power can be challenging in a world that believes only in what can be seen. Most of creation in unseen until the moment it manifests physically.

What is allowance?

Allowance is surrender. Surrendering to the belief that who or what we've allowed ourselves to be is a speck compared to the unlimited, creative beings we truly are. Allowance is surrendering to the knowledge that being of service through using our gifts and talents is one important way to express our creative power, and our connection to divine energy.

Allowance is knowing that life is meant to be lived fully, accepting all our experiences as divine and soul inspired. Our creativity is our gift to the world, as the ability to create is God's gift to us. In fully using our gifts, we honour ourselves and the ultimate creative source.

So what holds us back?

Sometimes it's believing we must do it all ourselves, thinking we are separate and must achieve in a manner the world agrees with. This fosters an environment in which we compare ourselves to others. Unfortunately there will be someone or a situation which provides us with proof that we are not the best.

There is only one thing we can be best at and that is being ourselves, believing in our talents and more importantly our dreams.

Kings Park, Winnipeg

A strong feeling of self-worth opens infinite possibilities to creating the life we desire.

When we hold onto our dreams we'll find ourselves in situations which present an opportunity to fully express our creativity. These situations will align themselves and the universe (i.e. our universe) will move in step with us. It is then we will realize it always did but we were not aware. It's like getting a new car; suddenly we notice more of them on the road than we previously thought existed.

One of the gifts of allowing is increased awareness, which happens because we no longer look for things to be a particular way but are open to all possibilities. We remove the blinders and see a broader view of our world.

Lack of self-worth limits our possibilities.

When we feel worthy and self-assured, life seems to adapt itself to our desires, seemingly by magic. We've all had the experience of wanting something so badly we feel we are not complete without it. We pray with conviction, focus intently and put most of our energy into acquiring it, and it may seem as though nothing is happening. Yet, when we relax and move on, it suddenly shows up. This is the basis for the statement, "Let go, and Let God".

We must have enough faith in our connection to life that there is no doubt what we desire will be manifested in our lives. When we doubt ourselves, we vacillate over the steps we must take, and this slows us down.

Divine power aligns with our most dominant thoughts and beliefs. If we hold the positive outcome we desire and know that the universe is blending the elements of our vision, life has no choice but to manifest what we desire into our lives. This is our creative power and the biggest challenge we face is faith and trust in the process.

A positive outcome will happen when we believe the result we desire can be achieved. The stronger our belief, the more effortless it will seem. This doesn't mean we will not have to work for it but the process of creation will not seem like work. It is then regardless of the effort required, the energy will be available from within. What we previously considered work will seem like play.

So to allow our creative power to contribute in a positive way in our lives, we must trust in our abilities, believe in ourselves, and allow the spark of God within to show its face to the world. To allow our creative power to be part of our everyday experience, we must be grateful and rejoice in the beauty of what we can create. We can then look back and marvel at what is possible when we allow our connection to the divine to be our guide, and know that faith and trust in the process is part of our contribution to life.

Brooklyn Bridge, New York

Boundaries

Boundaries are the guidelines we set for our lives. They determine the quality of our experiences.

Boundaries say to the world, "This is what I will accept and what I won't accept." They are part of the outward representation of how we think of ourselves, expressed as positive or negative beliefs, thoughts and actions.

When we do not have boundaries or unclear ones all types of negative experiences can appear.

Such an experience may show up as:

- The "friend" who sometimes takes advantage of us.
- The parent who cannot be strong for their children through wanting to be their friend.
- The lover who abuses us mentally, emotionally or physically.
- The worker who gets all the undesirable jobs and cannot stand up for him- or herself enough to say no.

Boundaries are the "NO" part of our lives that can produce positive experiences. When we set clear boundaries, our communication improves. If someone asks us to do something we are uneasy about, and we have clear enough boundaries, we can say no without feeling the need to explain or apologize.

In our daily lives we make numerous decisions, and each decision is determined by our beliefs.

On the positive side, boundaries declare to the world the confidence we have in ourselves and our ability to make good choices.

When we know what we desire in life, life has no choice but to make it part of our reality. We are continually working towards a goal whether we realize it or not. Our ability to reach our goals is determined by the boundaries we create, whether we develop them in childhood or later in life.

cont'd

Boundaries declare to the world the confidence we have in ourselves and our ability.

When we have clear boundaries we can say:

- No to drugs. (Really).
- No to having someone treat us in a way that is not good for our emotional, mental, physical or spiritual health.
- No to anyone coercing us into doing something illegal.
- No to ingesting anything in our bodies that is not conducive to good health.
- No to hurting another person intentionally.
- No to allowing the negative words of others to affect how we think about ourselves.

And what can we say yes to?

- Having a loving, supportive, nurturing and mutually giving relationship with everyone in our lives.
- Helping others when we can as long as it doesn't hurt us to do so.
- Experiencing an adventure which allows us to expand our currently held beliefs about ourselves.
- Allowing others to help us when we need it, and recognizing when we do.
- Seeing the beauty in each moment even the ones which may cause pain.
- Taking care of ourselves physically, mentally, emotionally, and spiritually.

When we cannot set clear guidelines in the form of boundaries, we tend to attract the things that cause ill health. These are manifested as addictions to people, things, substances, and experiences that cause us pain.

Ultimately, having boundaries builds the structure of our inner selves, where our deeply held beliefs are mirrored back to us in the form of our experiences.

If there is a part of our lives that is not working, living within the discipline that comes from clear and strong boundaries, will help create our most desired reality.

Living with joy comes from knowing that our experiences are part of our own creation. If there is someone in our life who is causing us pain, it is because we allow it.

When we truly love ourselves, we will erect the boundaries that keep our lives moving in the direction of our most desired reality.

Grow with grace and find union with the divine within, through love.

Assiniboine Park, Winnipeg

The whole has to support its parts to exist and to continue expressing itself as the whole.

Expectations

Having expectations about a thing is being tied to the outcome and thus moves us away from creating authentically.

Our expectations in effect say I do not trust and therefore I want it to be created in a particular way. Creating from our spirit involves knowing, and knowing bypasses expectations. Expectation says it doesn't exist for me. Our life experiences can only present what we believe is possible.

Knowing is beginning with the end in mind, and says I do not have to handle the details; I create the picture. Our vision of an endpoint involves knowing what we desire. When we intend or believe in an outcome, we are stating that it already exists. This allows the energy which forms the universe to align itself with our intentions and create the steps that get us there.

To create miracles all we do is speed up the time from conception to creation. Every one of us creates – that is all we can do.

When we say we want a thing, our wanting says it doesn't exist, and if we want for a long time we may eventually get frustrated and give up. Yet in most cases, the energy we've put into wanting is converted into creation when we relax and give up control of the process. The energy we've expended does not end. Our energy and thoughts live forever. What holds us back from instantly creating what we desire is the lack of belief we have in our ability to create.

Desire magnifies what we want, and this magnification aligns the energy necessary to manifest what we desire. Desire is an emotion that produces a higher level of creative energy than wanting.

Mayaro, Trinidad

It's no irony that for both our experiences and electricity we use the terms positive and negative. Both are the same energy manifesting in different forms.

Emotions are energy in motion. When our emotions are partnered with our intention we connect with the invisible force that is always in the motion of creation. Our thoughts or positive intention (if that is how our thoughts are) will align with similar thoughts, and together when enough energy is built up, our intention then materializes. (Many times a new scientific breakthrough happens in more than one place simultaneously, even if the people who come up with the ideas live great distances apart.) This is how we create, and whether we accept it or not is irrelevant because the energy of our thoughts will create in our lives, always.

Our power lies in clarity, and our challenge is to think positive thoughts, because creation works whether we're thinking positively or negatively.

Electricity is a form of energy. It is generated by millions of free-flowing electrons whose movements create force fields and generate energy from motion. We are a storehouse of electrical impulses and if we learn to move them in the direction of our desired reality through positive thoughts, we can use its power to create the life we desire. Because most of our thoughts are focused on negative outcomes, we shouldn't be surprised when we create negative results.

We are generally unaware of our thoughts. When we are aware, we see everything that occurs as contributing to Life. We accept all that occurs and know that an outcome is always created, and is necessary for Life to continue. Life is expanding and we are part of Life. Our lives are projections of the thoughts we hold most often within, so to create positive outcomes we must make positive choices, consciously.

So move beyond expectation and into knowing, because God and Life have no choice but to provide us with the manifestation of our thoughts. When we ask God and Life for help, they have no choice, because the whole has to support its parts to exist and to continue expressing itself as the whole. If Life is to continue expanding as it must, so too must each part. The highest expression of each part benefits the other parts, thus the whole.

Therefore for Life to continue, it has no choice but to provide us with our desires and intentions. Share your beauty, share your light, for that is the purpose of each part, shining brightly so the other parts can share their own light and brighten the world for all. This is how Life supports Life.

The solution to any problem we face exists within.

Being

To be, we must go beyond our current way of experiencing life. I see "BE" as beyond expectations. Our expectations have built-in limits. The very act of expecting a specific outcome limits all other possible outcomes.

The divine energy that forms the universe includes all that was, is, and ever will be.

Great thinkers and inventors are able to transcend the limits of current thinking to imagine other possibilities. Imagination is the tool we all have to start the creative process.

Einstein's theories would not exist if he focused on currently held limiting beliefs. The concept of relativity already existed on another level of thought. He was able to enter that realm of existence where all things are possible. If we could see through his eyes, it would be like looking at a movie and seeing all possibilities. The challenge comes from recognizing the ones which contain the solution to our most pressing challenge.

When we are focused exclusively on doing we stay trapped in our own world, with all of our prior experiences and present limitations.

A much greater world exists, where we can become the observer and see the intricate beauty and symmetry of our world. It's a place where all parts are interwoven with such precision that billions of worlds exist in harmony each and every second.

Imagine the enormity of the intelligence necessary to make this happen. If we were connected to this exquisite power, how would we live? We are in fact part of this power, with the ability to utilize it at will to create what we desire.

When we are aligned with this power a synergy exists, and we realize that all that is necessary is an acknowledgement of our part, our connection to this divine energy.

We utilize this power by being clear about what we desire. This clarity is attained through our imagination. When we meditate and quiet the chatter from the outside world, we enter an inner world that is connected to All That Is. It is here we experience that "eureka" moment – the flash of insight that exists, waiting for us to vibrate at the same frequency.

Within us, we all have the same capability that Einstein had. We are capable of utilizing this power to achieve more than we've ever thought possible.

However our highest achievements cannot be reached by doing alone, we must connect and align our power to the power that orchestrates the universe. To connect to this power we must take time to be. This takes us Beyond Expectations and into magic.

What do I feel I am Missing?

If I remember the divinity within and who I truly am, I will know I need nothing. There is no-thing I am not a part of. And if I feel that I need this no-thing I only have to remember that within me contains the everything that I AM.

We are complete but most of the time we live with illusions we call reality. We are here to create with awareness. Therefore, by imagining there is something we are not or there is something we do not have, we can then re-create ourselves into a new version of who we think ourselves to be.

We think our lives are real but the truth is we think it all into being. Thoughts create action, leading to the creation of matter, which we then assess and sometimes pass judgment on. We can then recreate by thinking again about what we have created.

Pain and disillusionment come when we judge what we've created as bad. But bad is an illusion; creation just is. However some of us may need the impetus that feeling bad creates, and that is okay. For as long as we believe that pain and suffering are catalysts to change, we live our illusions as the gifts for which they were intended. When we accept our pain with love, not condemnation nor resistance, we see its true purpose in our lives, and transcend our current limiting thoughts and beliefs to create ourselves anew.

This is the process of remembering who we are, and has been likened to peeling off layers to get to the core. We are not so much peeling off layers as we are putting together parts of ourselves to form our place within the whole that some call God or universal energy.

Without silence between notes music loses it's beauty.

We are part of the energy that creates and exists in all life.

Even the analogy of peeling off layers can help us understand. Peeling off layers brings us eventually to the core, which can help us realize we are nothing and everything.

We are everything in that we are part of the same energy which exists in all life.

It's like music. Without the silence between the notes, music loses its beauty. One cannot exist without the other.

What we fear contains within it the capacity for love. Our fears help us realize what we're not, which can then guide us to what we are. However even this is only partially correct for it assumes there is something we are not.

The essence of who we are is life. In thinking we are 'less than' or there is something we are not, we can imagine a different reality, where we fully appreciate the beauty of our divinity, and embrace our creative abilities.

To live the life of our dreams, our imagination must be used. To transcend our current limiting beliefs, we must be open to the divine within us that is not limited by the illusions we create about life.

Life is creative.

A life fully lived is one in which the individual is in a constant state of conscious creation. Our sense of who we are is transformed through our creativity.

Matlock, Manitoba

*Our light and our shadow and the illusions
we create form the structure of our lives*

Life

As I struggle day to day I ask myself "What am I doing?" What does my life mean? How are my experiences interwoven into this mosaic of life?

My light and my shadow and the illusions I create form the structure of my life.

Each experience can enrich my being or cause me to move further away from the love inherent in my life. It is inherent because it is my right by birth. Love is who I am unless I create the illusion that love doesn't exist in its richest form in my life. There is nothing I must do to deserve it or earn it.

How do I earn something that is so much a part of who I am it is impossible to separate me from it? I can only do this by creating the illusion that I am separate from life.

My beliefs about life are what I will experience. All my beliefs have created the me of today. If I do not like a part of me, I create an imbalance, and it's out of this I begin to create my own state of hell. God is in our "good" experiences and our "bad." God is all that is, and because of this we must embrace all our experiences.

Inner peace begins with the acceptance of our true selves and love for all things that occur in our lives. My realization is that loving the so-called bad that happens to me allows me to use my power to remember my divinity. The divinity within expands my world through love.

Therefore, to live according to the highest of the divine plan I am creating, I accept with love all that occurs. I open my heart, embrace all, and know that God lives within me and all that I meet.

When my tormentor comes, and surely he must, I thank God for arriving to show me how much I've remembered – how love can transform my vision of who I am and all my brothers and sisters. God has sent me someone who can be a light onto the darkness I refuse to see within.

When I meet people who challenge me, I thank them for they show me a reflection of myself, a momentary glimpse of what I could be.

When I meet those who curse me, I thank them for they show me how much love I can hold within.

When I meet people who slow me down, I thank them for they remind me to take time to breathe in life, deeply.

When I meet those who do not see me the way I see myself, I thank them for they remind me there is more beauty within, waiting to be revealed.

I thank God for visiting me in all forms good or bad, and the reminder that life is not a serious game but a joyful celebration.

Re-mind Yourself

You cannot experience anything differently than your self-concept. The idea you have of yourself is constantly creating your life.

If you believe you are smart then your experiences will reflect that.

So how do you change your idea of yourself and who you are?

Gratitude and imagination.

When you give thanks for life, you honour your being. You silently communicate to everyone you meet that you are a divine being creating a wonderful human experience. You see everything as a part of life, and since you are grateful for life, you embrace all your experiences and manifestations of life.

No life that's ever existed has been without challenges. Challenges come in all sizes and in all forms. There are two things of which you have no direct control over, your birth and your death. Everything in between is your creation, and while you may believe you do not directly control your experiences, each one is an opportunity to re-mind yourself.

When you re-mind yourself, you change your mind about the limitations you've accepted about yourself thus far in your life. Put another way, you remember the infinite possibilities you brought with you at birth. A child is not limited but sees the world (small as it is to them) as a vast playground with numerous opportunities to explore.

Limits are not part of a child's experience. Limitations are taught. The tool for teaching limitations is belief. As you grew older you were more often told what you can't do rather than what you can. Your "can't" became beliefs, and because it's not possible to act outside your deeply held beliefs, your limitations became your life.

Kakabeka Falls, Ontario

We are always connected to our source with the right to use that power to create our heart's desire

This is where the gift of awareness is valuable. Use your awareness so you can identify and transform beliefs that hold you back.

Your beliefs become filters through which every experience passes. The parts of the experience that do not fit your beliefs are discarded, not even noticed, and this you call reality.

Each time an experience fits your reality, your beliefs become stronger until they are cemented as knowing.

Think of those who are stubborn and have all the answers. Although it may be difficult, try to forgive them, for their beliefs create a separation and a constant battle. Their spirit's knowing and their human beliefs are in conflict, and so disharmony is created.

Accept who you are by embracing your spirit as your guide whose voice expresses itself as feelings.

Feelings aren't good or bad; their purpose in your life is simple. If a feeling is light, joyful and fun it is saying, "At this moment you are on a right path."

Conversely if a feeling is sad, angry, and guilty or any negative emotion, then it is saying, "In this moment, right now, the path you're on is not serving your highest good."

When you feel un-ease, your spirit is saying that change is necessary before your un-ease becomes dis-ease. So don't "dis" yourself. Accept the truth of who you are. Remind yourself that as part of the creative intelligence in all things, your connection to this power gives you the right to create your heart's desire.

As you follow your heart you live in alignment with your spirit (although you and your spirit are one), and remove the separation that dis-ease creates. You are always connected to your spirit, and the separation and limitations you may feel are merely illusions, for what is cannot not be.

An Honourable Life

If we cannot stand up for ourselves, no one else can. No one can do for us what we are not willing to do for ourselves.

When we love ourselves enough to accept only what is good for us and what feels good, we communicate the feeling of love to the universe and attract love back to ourselves.

We are beings of light. Light is necessary for life and we are life personified. Light connects us to everyone and everything.

Each experience we have is an opportunity to know and accept this. We are no better than anyone or anything. We are like a drop in the ocean of life, intermingled, each representing a part – but the whole cannot exist without its parts and the parts cannot exist without the whole.

Yet such is the cycle, for every drop that's taken out another returns. One of the best description I've heard that expresses our connectedness is by Deepak Chopra who said "Each of us is like a wave in the ocean, different, yet we cannot separate where the wave ends and the ocean begins." We are each similar parts expressing in different forms.

Like a storm in the ocean, the difficulties in our lives do not diminish us, they help define us. After each storm calm follows, but when the calm arrives, if we continue to focus on the storm we miss an opportunity to grow and truly experience and appreciate the goodness of life.

Open up, accept the storm for it can be the most enriching, life-affirming event we could ask for in this moment. It is then we can appreciate the calm, and put our efforts into transcending the difficulties the storm creates. We put back together what was broken down, and what we build is stronger and more beautiful than what the storm caused to be transformed. We grow and reach a higher level and appreciate our newfound level of strength. We discover new abilities, and find we are more than we thought ourselves to be.

Therefore when life gets difficult, appreciate it, because it's in growing through our difficulties that life expands. We see things and abilities that were always there but never noticed, and realize that life is a constant process of creation and recreation.

Life and living cannot end. When this part of our journey ends, it is only a crossroad, and on the other side is a new leg of our journey, a continuation which has but a different map.

At your crossroad look back on this part of your journey and see the potholes and the pitfalls and all the things you called negative and give thanks.

Of the millions of potential beings at conception, you were chosen to embark on this journey and that is the highest honour you could be given – to be born as you.

Connecting with Love

A Path to the Divine Within

Loving without conditions does not constrict, it expands. The people we love deeply and sincerely, we allow the freedom to BE anything they desire to be. We may sometimes feel there is not enough love in our lives. But that feeling is based on the limitations we may be experiencing in that moment.

If we feel there is not enough love in our lives, then this feeling should guide us to give more love to others. Because love cannot be given if it is not felt, the only way to get more is to give more.

The difficulties we face with love are based on our expectation that a person has to give love according to their relationship to us. We all have a concept of how the love of a parent, child, lover, spouse etc. should be. But unless we accept that the another person's concept of love may be different from our own, we will not be satisfied with the love we get from them. They can only love their way, not ours.

We each have our own internal representation of love.

It is easier to create with love than fear, except when we've become so used to the look of fear it's face is more familiar to us.

Creating A Life Of Love

Know yourself to be what you truly are, a magnificent creator, for you create everything in your life. Choose to live with grace, and choose love as your guide.

Creating with love begins with love for yourself. You cannot give what you do not have. If you feel that love is not a part of your life then that is what you will express to others.

Having a divine relationship means you consider yourself a divine being. When you keep this in mind, your actions will reflect your belief that all others you meet are also divine, and your divinity will connect you on a higher level with love.

You recognize your connection to life as an inspiring force that can transcend time or any other limitations you think may exist. All limitations you experience are of your own creation, and is based on all illusion of lack.

It is easier to create with love than fear, except when you've become so used to the look of fear that it's face is familiar to you.

Open your heart to loving yourself and others, and watch the manifestation of your dreams and desires in a way you could only imagine.

Black Rock, Tobago

We are individuals in this dance called life. We each take our own steps and when we move together it is beautiful.

To my Cherished One with Love

Your love does not complete me but expands me. I am me and you are you; we are individuals in this dance called life. You take your steps, I take my steps, and when we move together it's beautiful.

The way your body moves captivates me. I see grace even if others do not.

When you stumble, I smile because I see someone who can use my hand.

When you laugh, a well opens inside me, an outpouring of appreciation happens, and my world is brighter.

When you cry, I feel comforted because you show me you care, and that enriches my world.

When you smile, I see a vision that says you see something special, and if at that moment you are looking at me, my world is a much sunnier place.

When you hold me, everything stops and I thank God and appreciate the moment. It is then I think, "Life is good."

Your beauty is not in the clothes you wear, but the feelings you express.

And the universe speaks and I give thanks, for in that moment the beauty of life shows itself.

When I'm with you, life slows down and I appreciate all that you are, and love you more for sharing your life with me.

If only for that moment, my life expands and I will never be the same, and I thank you.

True love begins with self.

The Gift of Love

Living mindfully, with awareness and focused on the present is difficult for most of us. We try different methods – take classes, meditate – all to help us see and experience the power available when we live in the moment. Our efforts are usually designed to eliminate the effects and impact fear has in our lives. Fear's effects, while powerful, pale in comparison to the immense power of love.

Love is a very powerful emotion, yet most of us are more familiar with the emotions fear creates within us. Fear restricts while love expands. The expansion of who we are is what our spirit is guiding us to, even when we are not aware. Awareness creates within us the yearning to expand into the powerful beings we instinctively know we are.

Love and fear are both energy. Both use our emotions to expand our thoughts into material reality. Emotion is the engine; thought is the driver.

The quality of our lives is based on the conscious or unconscious thoughts we choose to direct our actions.

Fear and love by themselves are not creative; both are pure energy. This energy resides within us waiting to be guided in the direction of our thoughts.

We have no control over the events of our past or those yet to come. Our past is known and therefore familiar to us. The power we give to our past can result in re-creating similar experiences if we are not aware of how we feel. Fear is created from our judgments and conclusions about our past experiences and future expectations.

Fear can rob us of both our present and our future. This occurs because we've lost control of the only time we have to create – the present.

When we live this way, we under-utilize our power. For how can we create something different when we don't think differently?

Love is powerful because it helps us to be attuned and highly aware of each moment, each experience we encounter. Love creates such a powerful energy within us, that our immune systems are enhanced, and our senses are heightened. We experience life in a new way.

When we are in love we feel more powerful, able to embrace anything life presents. This is why the person we love continues to have a major presence in our lives long after the initial feeling has passed.

When we first fall in love, we feel invincible; we can accomplish more in less time than we normally would. We are in touch with our inner selves in a much more intimate manner than we normally are.

We live without judgment, and we tend to forgive the perceived shortcomings in others with ease, even to the point of not seeing the shortcomings in the person we feel affection for.

The word "affect" means to have influence on or to effect a change. We are affected by each experience, yet do not say we feel affection for everything that happens, because some of our experiences are "painful."

By trying to distance ourselves, rather than embracing the affection in our painful experiences, we miss the opportunity to grow from them.

Everything in life affects us therefore we have an affection for all that occurs whether we accept it or not. How it affects us is determined by how we choose to perceive our experiences. When we love life, we see the positive in everything, our "pleasurable" and "painful" experiences.

Major disasters have both a positive and negative effect. While peoples' lives may be affected negatively, disasters create opportunities for construction companies and numerous other businesses and industries. The businesses that sell lumber or concrete or ones that demolish buildings – all will experience business opportunities they couldn't have imagined, and therefore will find the value of their businesses increased substantially. In each "tragic" event there is a potential for loss and gain.

Individually, our ability to live a happy life depends on how we choose to be affected by our experiences in each moment.

Remember the saying, "it's not the years in your life that count it's the life in your years." Our feelings of love are a powerful, creative gift that begins within, with the acceptance of all that occurs as part of our journey.

Things happen; it's the judgment we make that determines whether we live with happiness or sadness. The gift of remembering the times we've loved deeply can put us in touch with those feelings and the quiet, intense power we felt. We may desire to live more of our lives this way, and we can because those feelings are part of our being.

Even the loss of loved ones can be a gift if we choose to remember the positive impact they had in our lives and our loving connection to them.

When a loved ones passes, it doesn't mean we have to miss them because they're gone. We can cherish them because they've lived. If we choose to treat them with affection while they've lived, we will have less pain and fewer regrets, because truthfully, most of our relationships exist in our minds.

Grand Beach, Manitoba

*When we choose to live life as a gift, our ability to
love expands and creates more of itself.*

If we were to look at two people who spend most of their time together, the time they spend with each other is marked by extended periods of thinking about their jobs, hobbies, and other life experiences. We are rarely living fully in the moment with ourselves, never mind being fully present with our loved ones when we are in their company.

There is a saying my parents used when I was a child, which was mind yourself. That meant pay attention, think about what you are doing and decide whether you want to continue doing it.

Most of our relationships are based on what movies, books and others tell and show us we should feel. For most of us, the beginning of a romantic relationship is the most intense feeling of love we will ever have, yet may be based on what external influences tell us romantic love should be.

True love begins with self. When we love another we can only do so to the level that we can truly love ourselves, accepting our insecurities and fears. The level of acceptance we have of ourselves is the same we afford to the ones we love. In accepting our insecurities and fears, we realize their purpose in our lives is to guide us to a richer, fuller experience of self-love.

All of life is a gift. Peace within begins with accepting with love all that we experience. When we choose to live life as a gift, our ability to love expands and creates more of itself. Know there is a positive purpose in all our experiences, even those we call negative.

Be affected by life, live with love and affection for who we are. Remember, we are an important part of life, and life cannot and does not exist without us.

When we say "I love you", it means I love you my way and others can only accept it based on their own concept of love.

What does it mean to Love Unconditionally?

Our idea of love is shaped by our life experiences. It would do us good to understand our partner's concept and idea of love. For the ultimate in any relationship is to know each person's idea of what love means to them, and help them experience that within the union you've formed.

It is not possible to love in a way you are not aware of. Your life is based on what you know and believe. How much richer your lives could be if you would allow yourselves the room to expand your idea about your experiences. You have an experience, and based on your self-concept, you form a judgment and call it reality. Even this is okay. However conflict arises when you project your "reality" onto others.

Based on what you call reality, you expect others to act a certain way, and when they do not you have a problem, but it is your problem, not theirs. The area where this is most obvious is parent-child relationships.

Most would agree that parents want what is best for their children. However this can manifest in having expectations of what their children should be doing with their lives. Some parents expect their children to be the next great doctor, lawyer, inventor, etc., and try to force them into activities and studies to accomplish what they themselves could not.

When they do this, their children can be robbed of the opportunity to be all they can or are meant to be, and the parent-child relationship can be damaged.

When you have a conflict, it is not with the other person but with yourself. Your experience begins within and then is projected outward. You cultivate your actions from your thoughts, and that is right for you because it is your experience and life.

So what does it mean to love unconditionally? First it must begin with love for yourself; after that the rest is easier. To love yourself unconditionally, you must accept all that you are, with love, especially the parts you do not like.

The parts of yourself, your thoughts, ideas, actions and feelings you do not like are the very areas that allow you the greatest opportunity for growth and mastery of your life. By first loving yourself unconditionally, you can then offer the same to others.

What you feel projects out of you and attracts more of the same. Therefore, if you find a lot of conflict in your life, become aware of what you are projecting and how you feel.

Toco, Trinidad

The ability to go within and live with awareness is not a gift granted to a select few. No one person or group has a monopoly on being special as this only creates separateness, and separation is the cause of the greatest conflicts you see in the world today.

If you are all connected, how can you harm another? Fighting is like having cancer; the parts that are diseased (not at peace within themselves) will destroy or attempt to destroy the surrounding healthy cells.

When you accept yourself as you are, warts and all, you begin to truly love and live. Your life expands and all the turbulence around you cannot change that. Life presents you with the opportunity to love, and in the moments of your greatest trials you find the beginnings of your greatest peace.

You can only do this through love and acceptance of yourself as you are – and others as they are. One of life's greatest illusions is that there is anything you need to be, do or have outside of you to enjoy life. Know that within yourself you need nothing and there is no-thing you are not a part of, because the very thought of a thing connects you to it. Conflict tends to arise out of need, especially in intimate relationships.

One of the first lessons taught in most religions is the Divine needs to have you be a particular way to experience a happy life ever after.

Most religions teach that there are unchangeable rules that must be followed; otherwise you are living a life of sin. This causes you to judge yourself and others as sinners.

In thinking you are created in the likeness of God, it must follow that you also think God must be like you. This is not a bad idea if you think of a loving limitless God as opposed to a God who judges and condemns.

You are connected to each other and everything that exists, and because of this, every experience you have is also your brother and sister's experience. There is nothing you need to do to deserve love. Need arises only if you feel you do not have enough love for yourself, and that others must supply more.

Need nothing – desire it all. It is your world and you are the creator of it. Create it with love for self and others, and watch your awareness of the beauty in life expand in your reality.

Loving Unconditionally begins with
loving ourselves, unconditionally.

Saline Bay, Trinidad

Prayers ...
Communicating with the Divine

What is Prayer?

Prayer is one's effort to re-connect with the whole. Feeling separate is an illusion because we cannot be separated from who we are. We are all connected

The most powerful prayer is a prayer of gratitude, which brings the awareness that our connection to the whole makes us complete . Just as we are.

We are each like a drop in an ocean called life, the ocean cannot exist without each drop and each drop cannot exist without the ocean.

Guayguayare, Trinidad

A Prayer of Gratitude is the most powerful Prayer there is.

Prayer for Divine Love

Divine Spirit, help me feel your presence in my life at all times. Allow me to see and feel the God within, sharing myself and my creations as a gift from God, through me to the world. Help me remember the immense power within that I can use to heal my life, and share the bounty and blessings with others so they may find their own path to love. Thanks for manifesting my desires into my daily living, and experiencing life as a living prayer.

Prayer for Self Acceptance

Divine Spirit, help me find within myself the capacity to receive humbly your greatest gifts. Give me the strength to face life's greatest challenges, and to embrace my challenges as opportunities for growth. Allow me to recognize these fantastic opportunities to grow into the loving being that is my centre.

Help me to heal the places within myself where I have not accepted love. And help me to love all others as cherished members of your family, and to see the greatness that is in each one of us.

As I live each day, share with me your gift of awareness so I may recognize the love that is deep inside of me. Give me the strength to face each day with love, and recognize the beauty that is in everything and everyone.

I now embrace my higher being and life.

Prayer to know the God Within

Dear God, in each moment help me find You in me. The me that is an outward representation of my spirit within. The me that dreams my dreams. This limitless person I would like to be my waking companion, and be the representative of who I truly am. I desire to know the magician within as an expression of my divine nature, and to manifest itself in my daily life. May my actions show the spark of divinity that resides within me.

Awareness of my power, and belief in that power are the only limits to creating miracles in my life.

Prayer for Living Spiritually

Divine Spirit, help me develop the strength to commit to living spiritually. Give me the guidance to positively affect the lives of others and help them (when invited) to find strength and divinity within themselves. I know my spirit's grace is who I am, and is a legacy of my connection to All That Is. When life presents itself, help me remember that in whatever form it displays, I have the power within me to accomplish my highest ideals.

Life is all there is, and I accept that. Even though I may not recognize it, there is a great purpose in all that occurs. A full life is available to me when I accept my own power within.

Thank you for life, and the power to create a life of my own choosing. Help me to choose my creations with my spirit as my guide, and love the expression of who I am.

Prayer for Accepting Change

Dear Spirit, I know that change is constant and my resistance to change creates conflict and difficulty in my life. Help me embrace the changes in my life, and to live with awareness and the guidance of my spirit to accept life as it is presented.

Help me to see clearly the changes in my life, and embrace the expansion of life and living that it brings. Strengthen my connection to life and the knowledge that I am safe and loved in the arms of Divine Spirit.

Life is ever expanding and I am part of that expansion.

Thank you God.

Hwy. #67 - Manitoba

"I live with the idea that we create a better world for ourselves when each interaction we have with others, leaves them feeling better about themselves."

About the Author

Photo: James Cassamajor

Anthony Fernando is a professional photographer, author and spiritual healer.

Anthony's journey began in Trinidad where playing cricket and reading helped him escape the violence and bleakness of a fractured childhood. At 14, he immigrated to the Canadian prairies, where the promise of better times never materialized as home life got worse. Again, books offered solace from the cold and harsh realities. As he tried to "figure things out", Anthony turned to self-help books from the psychology section. He also realized that he would need to overcome his shyness and begin reaching out to people.

Photography became a way for Anthony to capture his vision of the world and what he could see and share it with others. Through his computer studies, photography was a passion. While Computer Programming helped him balance his thinking between the intuitive and logical, photography opened his mind to different perspectives and his heart to the uniqueness and beauty of people and places. As friends discovered his photos, they asked him to photograph weddings and special events. His hobby became a full-time career, as he balanced corporate gigs with his own artistic work.

Anthony reached a turning point in 2001 when his long-time marriage suddenly fell apart. The release for his emotions came through writing. The writing of questions led to answers, in a free-flowing form. He discovered that articulating thoughts helped him face the emotional upheaval of the separation and move to a place of growth and opportunity.

Words and images came together in the form of greeting cards, motivational posters and Uncomplicating Your Life. Throughout his journey, Anthony has never allowed the bad things in his life push him to a place of hatred or stay in a place of anger very long. He looks for ways of not only getting through challenges but rising above them. His creative tools continue to nourish his spiritual healing and those around him.

email: info@uncomplicatingyourlife.com

website: www.AnthonyJFernando.com

        www.uncomplicatingyourlife.com

View additional photos: www.yourbestshot.ca

Greeting cards: www.momentsmatter.ca

Notes

Notes

www.ingramcontent.com/pod-product-compliance
Lightning Source LLC
Chambersburg PA
CBHW041524220426
43670CB00002B/24